TIME IN

TIME IN

Teaching Social Skills
in the Classroom

RUSTY MAY
&
TAMMIE ERICKSON

iUniverse, Inc.
Bloomington

TIME IN
Teaching Social Skills in the Classroom

iUniverse books may be ordered through booksellers or by contacting:

iUniverse
1663 Liberty Drive
Bloomington, IN 47403
www.iuniverse.com
1-800-Authors (1-800-288-4677)

ISBN: 978-1-4697-5806-0 (sc)
ISBN: 978-1-4697-5808-4 (ebk)

Library of Congress Control Number: 2012901224

Printed in the United States of America

iUniverse rev. date: 03/22/2012

Dedication

In loving memory of Sandy May and Kristina Acosta. You gave us the courage to be true to ourselves and the faith to believe that our words could help others.

CONTENTS

Introduction: Teaching Ourselves to Succeed ix

Chapter 1:   We Teach What We Need to Learn 1
Chapter 2:   Making and Breaking the Rules 8
Chapter 3:   What We've Lost 14
Chapter 4:   What We've Found 21
Chapter 5:   Making a Difference 32
Chapter 6:   Building Trust-Based Relationships 43
Chapter 7:   Respect 52
Chapter 8:   Responsibility 63
Chapter 9:   Resiliency 78
Chapter 10:   SchoolToolsTV 91

Postscript: A Conversation 102

INTRODUCTION

Teaching Ourselves to Succeed

Teachers and counselors are failing to give students the tools they need to succeed, not only in the classroom, but beyond. In this book, we offer our perspective on why this situation exists, and present some possible solutions.

"We" are Rusty May, an educator, coach, founder of SchoolToolsTV.com, and for several years, a middle school counselor; and Tammie Erickson, a fifth-grade teacher and mom. Together, we created this book to share our experiences and insights, earned over more than a decade working with real students in real classrooms.

Our purpose is to help teachers and counselors better understand and manage the issues we're facing in developing students' social skills. Each chapter, split into a "Counselor" and a "Teacher" section, offers pieces of our personal journeys and real-classroom experiences. We close the book with a dialogue between us that we hope will spark further conversations between counselors and teachers everywhere.

As teachers, we fail our students when we acquiesce to installing processes instead of developing relationships. We fail our students when we don't see ourselves as human beings in a classroom full of other human beings. We fail our students when we spend more time on our lesson plans than we do in becoming more aware of who we are and how we connect with others.

As counselors, we fail our students when we give in to our need to be liked by a student over the needs of the classroom teacher. As counselors, we fail our students when we make excuses for one who is struggling, despite the reality that awaits a child who has been coddled through to graduation. As counselors, we fail our students when our thought processes become more about how we're perceived instead of holding students accountable for bad behavior and poor decisions.

Succeeding as a teacher or a counselor requires much more than a grasp of the educational material; it's about understanding our own strengths and weaknesses and remaining calm in the face of adolescent angst. It's about connecting with students at a level where they feel safe and empowered to take risks and bond to us, the leaders of this transformational process. Teachers need professional development to become more self-aware, and training to create effective learning relationships in the classroom. They also need counselors who regularly work with them, to keep this aspect of their professional lives healthy and growing.

Counselors need to focus on the teacher-student relationship because students must be successful in the classroom, not the counselor's office. Counselors need to be a resource for the teacher more than a friend to the child. Students don't need adult friends; they need people who lead by example and hold the bar at the right height. With very few exceptions, the work of the school counselor should be to empower the teacher and to support the effort to create a learning community in each classroom, as well as a culture of excellence and high expectations throughout the school.

Some believe that teachers fail because they don't have a mastery of the subject matter, so they can't bring math and science to life. However, the developmental process of the adolescent brain must be taken into consideration. The student who sits in a classroom during a lecture is often incapable of grasping the true nature of the information being presented. Worse, that child rarely feels a personal connection with the teacher. Those two factors exacerbate one another in a cycle of indifference and missed opportunities for the students as well as the teachers.

Many of us found our way in life because of teachers who saw us as we were, and then sold us on the idea of what we could become. They cared for us enough to let us fail, and believed in us enough to let us fall. They pushed us, even when doing so brought our resentment down on them and their efforts. Their "tough love" approach was just what we needed. They cared about us more than those who simply told us that everything was going to be OK.

Students can see right through us; they can tell the difference between concern for them and concern for a pension. They know whether our efforts are about them as people who need to be improved or them as test scores that need to be raised. We can spend years and billions of dollars making teachers better at delivering information, only to find at the end of the day that students, or anyone else for that matter, won't push through walls for people who they don't care about, and who they don't feel truly care about them. Most of the blank stares you're getting from your students are not because they don't get what you're saying. They get exactly what you're saying, and they know that it has more to do with what you need from them than what they need from you.

Scoring on large standardized tests determines a great many things in public school districts, but the dictatorship of "teaching to the test" creates a competition between teachers and students. In that competition, the teacher is judged by the product that the student produces, and the students are left to fend for themselves. The adults who should model and mentor appropriate behaviors for students are too focused on test scores to even see the needs of the whole student. We've lost the greatest thing about education, which is the teacher-student relationship. In sports, we call it buying into the system. It's the respect, trust, and belief, especially in the face of uncertainty, that allows a teacher or a coach to connect with a student.

Some of us, as young students or athletes, took actions out of faith and trust because we knew that our teachers or coaches wouldn't steer us wrong. These people cared about us and led by example. They didn't complain when things didn't go their way, and when they made mistakes they acknowledged the error of their ways and made it right.

Today, many of us have lost this ability. Often are we telling the students one thing about personal accountability, yet doing something completely different in our daily interactions at school. We tell our students to be nice to each other, and then we go into the teacher's lounge and trash talk the teacher down the hall or the principal's new policy.

We tell our students to work hard and never give up, and yet we openly complain about how hard our jobs are and how little we get paid. We tell our students that they need to get along with each other, but there's usually one kid in the class that we can't seem to get along with and they all know it. How stupid do we think they are? Students learn more from what we do than what we say.

Race to the Top, which is a federal program designed to spur public school innovation, is a race to nowhere unless we prioritize educational relationships and the connection between teachers and students. Professional development is a joke unless teachers and counselors begin to see themselves as the object of improvement. Einstein had a pretty good grasp of physics but he couldn't get a job because he failed to relate to students and their problems. K-12 students need our attention, and they need to know that we care. They need to know that we understand that we ourselves are all too human. They need teachers, not trainers.

The education that will prepare students for the reality of the 21st century is rooted in their ability to learn, unlearn, and relearn information seven or more times during the course of a normal working career. Technology is moving so fast that, in many cases, the jobs we're preparing our students for don't yet exist. Race to the Top and other educational reforms focus on the training aspect of skills acquisition, but training is akin to memorization. It is the ability to perform a task without even understanding that task's meaning or purpose. For the adult learner, training is acceptable. For the adolescent learner, however, it's all about meaning and connection.

Consider the very real issues of students who come from poverty and dysfunctional home environments. We know that early childhood trauma negatively affects a child's ability to attach and bond to people and situations. We know that these students have a hard time trusting others and that they lack the basic skills necessary to function effectively in the classroom.

We also know that these skills aren't being taught in most classrooms today. Instead, students are being punished for their lack of skills in ineffective ways, such as removing them from the classroom and sending them home to the place where the dysfunction often began. Even one or two of these students can consume a great amount of teaching time, and the result is often a reduction in test scores for the entire class. It's therefore no surprise that most teachers, when confronted with this situation, find it easier just to remove the problem students from the class and move on.

So what do we do with these students? We offer them up to special education and give them unrealistic accommodations and social promotion without consideration of what this will mean to their future possibilities. The truth is that there is no special education in the real world. We're only postponing the problem that we as a society will eventually have to deal with: Another generation reliant on the social system or subject to the penal system.

For the past 20 years or more, teachers have received professional development to more effectively disseminate information, all the while losing the ability to connect and attach to those they must teach. Teaching is not about disseminating information; that's training. Teaching is about relationships. I won't learn from you until I trust you, and I'm not going to trust you more because you send me to the principal's office or let me take time out of my day to play with the counselor.

Counselors, on the other hand, have been connecting with kids too much and thereby doing the students and the teachers a disservice. School counseling, especially at the elementary level, has become about befriending children and empathizing with their situation. Counselors have become protectors and fight for the student's right to use his or her upbringing as an excuse to underperform in the classroom or act out on the playground.

For many new counselors, the goal is to be liked by the students. We may want the kids to yell out our name when they see us in the hall or on the playground. It's not an uncommon emotion to want to be the one caring adult who could make the life-changing difference in the life of a disenfranchised student. We all want to be the safe place in school that kids can go and forget about their troubles for a while. Those sound like admirable goals, but that's not the job.

The job of the counselor is to help the teacher do his or her job. The job is to hold the bar high for clients and teach them the skills they need to be more successful in the classroom. The job is to work with teachers to help them notice their own blind spots with individual students, and provide supportive feedback so they can adjust and improve. The clients should be the teachers and the job is to create functional relationships that improve the school climate and meet the educational goals of each classroom. Counselors need to teach teachers how to build relationships with their customers, the students that they teach. Make no mistake about it; this is the bottom line in the educational debate. Students are our customers and the taxpayers are our board of directors. If we don't learn how to connect with our customers, we'll lose our schools.

The sooner we realize that relationships are the key to educational reform and begin to support the transfer of that responsibility to the classroom teacher, with the full support of the rest of the professional staff, the sooner we'll be moving forward again and giving our customers the skills they need to succeed in the 21st century.

Failure isn't an option. Together, let's see how we can succeed.

CHAPTER 1

We Teach What We Need to Learn

Counselor

I became a counselor to help people; I wanted to have the kind of positive effect on kids that the trusted adults in my life had on me. Being raised in a military family, we moved every few years. Besides my family members, the coaches and teachers I met along the way helped me acquire the basic skills I needed to make it to where I am today.

When I say basic, I mean basic. As I write this, I'm 48 and just now starting to feel like I've found my groove. I have struggled mightily with low self-esteem, anger issues, and poor impulse control. During my youth, my mentors gave me the gift of time and the aforementioned skills I needed to get through school and make a living in the working world. They also gave me the courage to never quit looking for my path.

These people weren't perfect. The sun didn't rise and fall at their feet. They were real people who cared about me as a person first and as a student-athlete second. I've been a basketball coach for years, and I now realize that it doesn't matter how much I know or how well I can impart that knowledge. If I can't connect with my players, I'll be average at best. Two stories from my youth illustrate this idea, and both involve the same man.

In 1976 my dad was transferred to Dyess Air Force Base in Abilene, Texas. Along with my older brother Charles and my sister Cathy, I went to Madison Junior High. Mike, the fourth sibling, went to Jackson Elementary. Bobby, the youngest, wasn't yet in the school system as he was just five at the time. We usually moved in the summer during the school break, which worked for me because it meant that I could try out for the football team before school started.

Football practice offered an opportunity to prove myself and make a few friends before classes began. My brother Mike has always said that I was a very good football player, but any success I experienced had less to do with talent and more to do with my burning desire to fit in. If I made an impact on the field, the rest would take care of itself. It was survival, plain and simple.

Abilene had about 100,000 people back then, and most had been born in the same hospital. I had to succeed in football; the only other choice was to spend the next two or three years on the outside looking in. Those of us trying out for the team weren't going to find out who made the cut until a few days after school started. During those first few days, I ate by myself or with Charles and Cathy when we had the same lunch period.

On one of those in-between days, the head coach of the team, a man by the name of Wiley Wise, was walking around the cafeteria, touching base with all of his players. Then he stopped, looked straight at me, and said, loud enough for everyone to hear, "Hey May, how's the food today?" It was all I could do to nod my head and try not to tear up because in that one moment, he connected with me on a personal level. In doing so, he instantly connected me with everyone else.

About a year later, I had another experience with Coach Wise that was very different but equally powerful. My friends and I snuck out on a Friday night, stole some beer from a garage, and drank until about 3 a.m. We had practice that morning at seven. As soon as I walked into practice, I knew we were in trouble.

One of my partners in crime had his helmet on backwards and was trying to tackle the line coach. When I made a catch during practice,

Coach Wise said, "Nice grab. I'm surprised you can even see the ball." I guess we weren't fooling anybody, and when practice was over, the coaching staff called me in.

I told them what had happened, and Coach Wise told me to get into his truck. He was going to drive me home. When we got home, he walked into my house, sat down with my parents, and told them what he had discovered. He then explained that he wouldn't cut me from the team, but that my compatriots and I would pay a heavy price after practice over the next few weeks. He thanked my parents for their time, and he went on his way.

What was so amazing to me was the fact that my parents left it at that. They knew that this man was going to make his point and they trusted their son with him. The next two weeks were the hardest of my life, but I knew that Coach Wise was doing it for me. It wasn't a punishment. It was a second chance. The lesson was that I, the whole person, was worth more than my actions.

These lessons and many others from Coach Wise stay with me to this day. In looking back, however, I realize there was much that my family, coaches, and teachers didn't teach me. It could have been because they were afraid to acknowledge my weaknesses, or because those weaknesses worked in their favor, like on the playing field. I come from a relatively functional family and went to schools where teachers didn't have to teach to the test. Yet despite these factors, I didn't have a clue how to deal with my anger and low self-esteem. My mentors and role models weren't much help.

One of the big advantages in getting my counseling degree was the amount of time we spent talking to each other about our problems. Many of my classmates were reluctant to open up, but I jumped in with both feet. I was old enough to know that my behaviors weren't working, and was hungry to discover ways to start enjoying some success. What I learned about myself through that experience was eye-opening. My thoughts created my anger? I had a choice about how I reacted to any situation? No one could make me angry without my permission? This information blew my mind.

During this process, I recall thinking, "Why didn't I learn this stuff in school? Why did I spend so much time ruining relationships because of my own insecurities and self-doubt?" It was simply because I didn't know any other way. No one taught me that there were any alternatives.

My mom kept all my report cards from those days, and she gave them to me a few years ago. I was amazed to find out two things. First, I was a good student. For some reason, I remembered myself as being average, but the truth was that I had As and Bs throughout school. The second surprise was a statement made by my kindergarten teacher, who wrote that I was a wonderful student but that I also had a very bad temper. She thought that I would need to learn how to deal with that or it would affect my ability to do well in school. Duh!

Everyone knew I had a problem, but no one knew how to deal with it. I was never taught to take deep breaths, or sent to a counselor to talk about my fears and resentments. I was left to my own devices and that didn't work. I needed help. Years later, when I started to see the light, I was sure I could help others, so I became a school counselor.

During my three years of training, I was told repeatedly that I would get very little of the teachers' time, and that I would have to rely on a 30-minute session once a week to give my clients the tools they needed to be more effective in the classroom. I remember thinking, "I've got this," and off I went.

Early on in the practical training, I realized that I was making connections with kids and that they looked forward to seeing me. I was able to create solids bonds with the vast majority of the kids in my care. However, I wasn't dealing with them in times of stress. They did well when they were with me, but often didn't know how to deal with frustration or authority figures that needed their attention.

Something was missing, and so I started looking for another way to help. I was writing my thesis at the time, and my professor told me to look for something at school that no one else wanted to do and develop that into my final project. The school at which I counseled back then had a daily video program, called Rosedale TV, where they made announcements and talked about upcoming activities. Each week, a different teacher was responsible for bringing in his or her class and running the show. I quickly learned that this was not the teachers' favorite thing to do. It required extra time in their already overloaded schedule, and most of them were not excited about being on TV first thing in the morning. I asked if I could take it over and write a curriculum to incorporate social skills in the daily message, and they gave me the keys to the kingdom.

The journey that followed taught me that to truly help classroom teachers, I needed to provide tools and prompts that they could use to create a bond with their students on a daily basis. Social skills and character traits, which were at least part of my educational experience as a young person, had fallen by the wayside in an age of teaching to the test. I wanted to create a way for teachers to address these issues, which would affect students' futures every bit as much as math and language skills. Thus, SchoolToolsTV was born.

We'll talk more about SchoolToolsTV in chapter 10, but suffice it to say that the program, as well as this book, represents my way of reaching out to those of you who know what the problem is but feel helpless when it comes to solutions. I want to give you permission to do what you know in your heart needs to be done: to connect with each student as if his or her life depends on it. In reality, it does.

Teacher

I wanted to be a teacher for as long as I can remember. Even as a young girl, I dreamed of grading papers, writing my name on the blackboard, welcoming smiling children into my classroom on the first day of school, creating amazing lesson plans that would take those same children far in life, and having them return years later to thank me. I could write an entire book about how most of those dreams became reality, but that is not what this book is about. This book is actually about the exact opposite—things that I never could have imagined would happen in a real classroom.

I have been teaching for 10 years, currently fourth graders in Billings, Montana. I've also taught second, third, and fifth grade. My career began in Palm Beach Gardens, Florida, just as No Child Left Behind (NCLB) became law. This Act of Congress was designed to create measurable goals for students, and tied federal funding for public schools into those assessments. As a result, there was (and is) immense pressure upon me, as on all teachers, to drill our students in the necessary academics so they can excel on standardized tests.

I accepted the challenge to teach to the test, signed on the dotted line, and got to work. I did my job very well. My test scores went up, my principal praised me, and I even earned a cash bonus. I also got the pleasure of watching, or should I say ignoring, my students throwing up, crying from migraine headaches, and searching in vain for some sign of support and human connection from me. I could only respond with the "teacher look" that told them that they darned well better pass this test.

Then, I learned I was pregnant.

My pregnancy provided absolute joy and a huge slap in the face. I started to question my future as a teacher, or at least, my current way of teaching. A strange feeling crept into my soul, one that I had worked very hard to shove down for two years. I felt empathetic, especially when I imagined my daughter's future as a student. I saw her throw up on test day, saw her beg to go home to sleep off a migraine, and saw her teachers give her a cold look that shot straight through to her soft, sweet soul when she was desperate for words of encouragement. I remember crying, and then coming to the realization that a dramatic change was needed.

I grew up in Montana, so the first change was to move back home. Life in Montana always seemed simpler, and simple was something I needed at the time. I applied for a position with the local school district, and was hired. I had a fresh start: new people, new attitude, new vision, new understanding.

As always, I believed (and believe) that academics are very important, but I also knew that kids are just that, kids. They are someone's daughter and son, and deserve to be treated with compassion and respect. Children need to learn many things, and some of these lessons fall outside the traditional subjects of reading, math, spelling, and science that are assessed through state testing. Kids also need love, the same love that filled my heart as a small child when I dreamed of becoming a teacher. I added a new column to my lesson plan book that year: character education. I didn't teach that column that year. Instead, I lived it over the next eight.

Two children, eight years, and a divorce later, I remain engaged in this amazing journey, this incredible, never-ending process of educating children to be good students and good citizens. A lot of that process is woven into the pages of this book. Am I where I want to be? If I were, I would have added the word "retirement" to my list of achievements. I am still growing, every single day. Have I come a long way? In my opinion, yes. Do I have a long way to go? Absolutely. The process changes daily. Just when I think I am on to something, the school year ends, and I get a new group of students. I then start all over, taking what I know and adding new components that match the style of my class.

Teaching is trial-and-error. It is years of self-reflection. It is sharing what you learn and what you believe with others. It is applying. It is never giving up. It is motivating others to join you. It is standing up for a child. It is understanding and patience. It is change. It is a little girl playing school in her basement, dreaming of making a difference in the world. It is me.

CHAPTER 2

Making and Breaking the Rules

Counselor

I was recently asked to do some work with an older teacher who was struggling with his third-grade class. After watching him for several weeks, it was obvious that he was teaching by the book. He had a zero-tolerance policy for misbehavior and a system in place to enforce it.

On a wall by the door, there was a bulletin board with a pocket for each student, and three colored cards in each pocket. The color cards were changed according to each student's compliance with the rules. For a first offense, the student's card changed from green to yellow, and he or she lost the next recess period. On a second offense, the card went to orange and the student was referred to the principal's office for a lecture and a call home. The third offense led to a red card and after-school detention. Students who did more egregious things were suspended. The cycle continued, day after day. This teacher was spending so much time with discipline and enforcement that it was impossible for him to complete even the most basic lesson plan. He eventually quit, caused partly by a nasty fall when one of the children he was trying to corral on the playground moved quickly to avoid his grasp, and partly because of his overwhelming sense of frustration.

In reflecting on this situation, what keeps going through my head is the old saying about the definition of insanity: "Doing the same thing over and over and expecting different results." This teacher had rules, he had consequences, and still some kids weren't getting it. As a result, he was spending a good deal of time dealing with those kids. I get the opportunity to visit hundreds of classrooms every year and all of them have some form of a discipline policy similar to the one I just described. Here is an example of a policy from a classroom I visit on a regular basis:

Classroom Rules
- The Golden Rule: Treat others the way you want to be treated
- Follow directions
- Respect asking for help. Wellness Wednesday talked about diet, exercise, respect school and personal property
- Use appropriate language
- Work and play safely (keep hands, feet and other objects to yourself)

If a student chooses to break a rule, the following consequences will apply:
- First time: warning
- Second time: loss of recess and an action plan
- Third time: removal from the room (time out) and a phone call home
- Fourth time: referral to the principal's office and a phone call home

The skills being asked of the students are ones that we take for granted, but are skills nonetheless. The negative consequences have nothing to do with skill development; they are intended to create a situation that the student wants to avoid, thereby making him or her abide by the rules. But what if that student has never been taught the skills in question? What if the student has no respect for authority? What if that student has no real relationship with the teacher? What if the student doesn't feel that these rules are about anything other than control?

Besides punishment, there are often no interventions to help students understand the value of skills such as these. Look at the list again. How did you learn to use appropriate language or play in a safe manner? Who taught you these skills? Did you have a positive, trust-based relationship with that person?

The rules on this list and thousands of others just like it on the walls of classrooms everywhere represent social skills and character traits that must be taught before they can be followed. The relationship that the teacher has with the student will be the most important factor in determining whether or not these rules are learned and embraced. Our current system has moved so far in the direction of the acquisition and dissemination of information that we've lost something very important in the teacher-student relationship. The students don't respect us anymore. They aren't going to follow our rules, and we can't make them. They know we can't, and we're starting to realize this, too. Game on.

Children are experts at reading us. They know the difference between real power and "authority," which is based solely on the threat of punishments that no longer work for most of those who "choose" to break the rules. I have kids that I work with who get into trouble on purpose whenever they want a break or a long weekend. They go home to televisions, video games, and almost nonexistent adult supervision. If they're struggling with a subject or are getting bored, they act up so they can go to the principal's office. Why would they want to do that? Well, they get to walk there and that's fun. Have you ever watched kids walk back and forth down the halls? They may not be interested in class but they are fascinated by every single thing that is posted in the hallway. Maybe we should post the lessons out there; that way, some of our more troubled kids will at least get a chance to really look them over as they take their daily 5-to 10-minute walks down to the most interesting place in the school: the main office. The office is full of sound and fury, and usually an adult or two will stop and talk to the kids who are waiting to see the principal. The principal is busy, so the kid gets to wait it out while listening to the phones ring and watching all the people fly by. The principal does his or her best to impart words of guidance and warnings of things to come. Then the student returns to the hallway, the class, and the same behaviors.

Why does this happen to so many students, time and time again? Because neither they nor we know how to do anything differently, and the system isn't set up to teach students how to be people of character. Schools are not teaching students the social skills they need to make it in the outside world, and teachers aren't creating the relationships necessary to accomplish their goals in the classroom. If we can change that equation, anything is possible; if we can't, nothing is.

Teacher

When I was a student, things were different. I remember sitting in my fifth-grade class one day as the teacher wrote my name on the front board as a punishment for talking in class. Later in the day, a check mark appeared next to my name for talking again. My name on the board was a warning, and the check mark represented the loss of five minutes of my recess.

This event sticks in my mind, and it did help modify my behavior, although it wasn't the loss of recess that worked—it was the horrifying thought that everyone else in the class saw me get into trouble, and anyone who walked into that classroom (teacher, guest, or, god-forbid, the principal) knew I was in trouble, too. There was a feeling inside me that went along with the consequence I was given. It was disappointment. I had disappointed my teacher, my class, my parents, and myself. It bothered me that I had made a negative choice and had to be held accountable for it.

This doesn't seem to be the case with today's students, who tend to see their choices linked with a consequence. The feeling of disappointment inside their gut is no longer present. They just want to know if a particular behavior is going to lead to a specific punishment, and get it over with. They apologize only after being prompted. I often find myself repeating the definition of the word, "Sorry" in my classroom. I say, "Sorry means that you will try your very best to not let this behavior happen again." They agree, but do they really understand those words? In my experience as a teacher, I have seen many, many repeat offenders. It is as if they have no control over their own behaviors and choices.

Writing this book has allowed me to realize that I learned right from wrong from my parents and teachers, mostly because I was scared that they would form negative opinions of me. The worst punishment ever given to me by my mother was for her to look me in the eye and say, "I am very disappointed in you, Tammie." Ouch! So, I began to make choices that would lead me away from consequences in which I would hear that phrase.

One consequence I do not remember ever hearing about when I was a kid was the zero-tolerance policy. The realities that contribute to the making of this policy barely existed when I was a child. Drugs, weapons, and life threats were extremely uncommon in my generation in Montana. After events such as the Columbine massacre, administrators had to take proactive roles in preventing similar occurrences.

Zero tolerance to me means one strike and the student is out. It means no warning, no lunch detention, no phone call home. It means you committed a particularly troubling act, and now you are done: kicked out of the school, clean out your locker, good-bye. So, this is how I taught it and explained it to parents. However, I've come to find out that this is not what it means. Zero tolerance really is just a name for a systematic approach, relying mostly on consequences, to deal with behaviors such as drug use, weapon possession, bullying, and threats. I was shocked when I discovered that students were given warnings, detention, and suspensions for these behaviors and were back in my classroom a few days later, often looking at me with no remorse in their eyes. They even sometimes bragged about everything they got to do during this mini-vacation. It seemed to me that the punishment did not fit the crime, and that the wrong lessons were being learned. It also left me wondering, "Where is the parent in this situation?"

I recall one particular instance in my fifth-grade classroom in Florida. One of my students became angry when I asked him to complete a task. He said no and received all the negative attention, gasps, and snickers from his peers that he desired. I continued to calmly request the correct behavior choice again. To this he replied, "F—you." I will never forget that day. I was absolutely in shock. I had seen this type of behavior in the movies, but never in a million years did I believe it would happen in my own precious classroom, from a pre-teen no less.

After my shock wore off, I called the office to have the child removed. Another staff member arrived and removed the boy from my class. I remember thinking, "I will show you who is boss in this situation." However, about 15 minutes later, the boy returned to my class, took his seat, and slyly smiled at me. He had won; I had lost my authority. He had singlehandedly destroyed my reputation as a teacher in front of the entire class. I was angry with him, but I was also angry at my administration for the way they handled the situation. I vowed to myself that day that I would never again send a child to the office for an infraction I could handle myself.

So, I waited for the day that this particular little boy would challenge me again. I knew it would come, and it did. The same type of situation occurred. He became defiant and used inappropriate language again. This time, I gave him no reaction. I simply stated that I could tell that he was upset and asked him if he needed a cool-off period. I told him he was welcome to go get a drink of water or walk down the hall and just take a break. I told him that this was a strategy I often found helpful in my life when I became upset. He still refused to do the work that day, but I regained my dignity and position of authority, and did it in a respectful way. Time after time, I modeled this strategy to this little boy that year. I hope he applied this lesson later in his life.

CHAPTER 3

What We've Lost

Counselor

How did we get here? It's a combination of societal forces and a change in the teacher-student relationship. On the one hand, society is less tolerant of harsh disciplinary strategies that force student compliance, parents are less involved in the educational system in general and their kids' lives specifically, and the respect that children (especially students) once demonstrated to adults is no longer a given. On the other hand, teachers have to work within a test-based environment that creates an impression that training, not relationship-building, is only thing that matters.

I grew up in a time and place where the phrase, "Spare the rod, spoil the child" was taken as faith. My parents believed in strict punishment, and the system did as well. I went to Catholic schools where the nuns were very proficient in the use of rulers whenever I or any of my fellow students stepped out of line. Later I experienced the paddle on a regular basis in the public schools I attended in the South. I strongly disagree with these strategies but they did have an immediate effect on my behavior. I wasn't learning how to do anything differently, but I was afraid of getting hit and that was enough to keep me compliant most of the time.

Using force to solve problems in the classroom creates children who do the same when they face an obstacle. My experiences led me to believe that a show of force was the way to regain control, and that learned behavior has ended up costing me a great deal in my life. Anger, guilt, and shame inhabited me from early youth into adulthood. I had no idea how to handle these emotions until I began to acquire the skills of personal honesty and mutual respect. That allowed me to view problems as something to be solved instead of something to force my will upon.

The pressures and demands on today's parents severely limit their ability to stay involved in their child's education. This often prevents parents from following through at home on disciplinary actions that occur at school. When I was a child I didn't want to get suspended because there was a very real price to pay at home if I did.

First of all, my mom didn't work, so that meant I would be supervised for the entire time. When I got up in the morning, I was allowed to eat breakfast, and then I spent the rest of the day on my bed doing schoolwork or reading. I was not allowed to go outside or watch TV, and even after I returned to school three days later, I was still on restrictions at home that limited everything I did for the following two weeks. A large number of today's most challenged students do not have that type of system in place at home to reinforce the consequences that occur at school, and so suspensions are ineffective.

There is also a growing "respect gap" between adults and children. The students I work with tend to see very little difference between themselves and "tall" people because they are not exposed to many functional adult relationships outside of school. Naturally, they bring that reality into the classroom. In addition, some parents want to befriend their children, and this also tends to widen the respect gap.

I was not raised like this. I was raised to say, "Yes sir" and "No ma'am." Adults drew a very distinct line in their relationship with me. I am not here to criticize or to join the long line of people who believe that we need to go back to move forward. This is where we are and these are the issues the modern day teacher and counselor must face. However, the first step in solving a problem is to name it.

Meanwhile, the role and expectation of the teacher has changed. The teachers I grew up with had more flexibility in their use of time, and due to the parents' involvement and support, these teachers became more like a part of the family during the time that we were in their classrooms.

Today's teacher has blocks of time that must be used for specific educational instruction. They are constantly aware that they will be judged by the test scores that their students receive. Teachers are expected to not only teach, but also to manage a group of 20-30 students, guiding them in the direction of excellence, following the rules and consequences mentioned in chapter 2.

We end up with students who don't have the basic social skills needed for effective learning to take place, and teachers who are not given the tools they need to create that kind of change. Making matters more complicated, these teachers might not keep their jobs if their students don't do well enough on the testing.

The students are very aware of this duality of purpose. Most of the kids I've worked with over the years have mentioned at one time or another that their teacher doesn't really care about them, only their test scores.

Think about how you school prepares for Red Ribbon Week, versus how much time and energy goes into preparing for the two to three weeks of testing. I've been at schools that hung posters and tied ribbons in the last week of October, but we had pep rallies, guest speakers, movie rewards, extra recess, game shows, free snacks, and bottled water during testing in the spring. The students know how important the tests are, and they know that the teachers are keeping one eye on that outcome from the very first day of class.

Many particularly challenging students are leading lives that also serve to push them and their teachers apart. Many of these kids come from some pretty dark places, and teachers have confided in me that they have a hard time hearing the stories that their students tell, and are often frustrated in their attempts to involve Child Protective Services.

Teachers tend to be very empathetic, and they often take their work home with them. Counselors, who have been trained to deal with these types of issues, are encouraged to regularly attend debriefing sessions with their team members as a way of helping them cope with some of these issues. Teachers don't have this support system in place. It is therefore much easier to focus on the business of education and leave the emotional development to someone else, like a counselor (if the school is lucky enough to have one).

The American School Counselor Association recommends a ratio of one counselor for every 250 students. According to recent studies, the national average is 469 to 1; in my home state of California, the ratio is 814 to 1.[1]

The counseling model in education has the majority of its resources at the high school level, which is focused mainly on academic issues and crisis management. Middle schools often have one or two counselors, leaving very few in the elementary schools. Most of the schools that I work with have a budget for a school psychologist, but these professionals focus mostly on academics.

Having said all this, I've come to realize that even if we had a better system in place and more resources to go around, the fact that the child can bond with me during a 30-minute session one day a week doesn't always translate to a better relationship between that student and the teacher in the classroom.

So here we are. We have limited effective consequences, limited parental support and follow through, and limited time and resources. Meanwhile, we're facing students who lack the basic social skills needed to follow the rules in the classroom, and who know that the teachers need them to do well on the test to keep their jobs.

The question becomes, "Do we keep doing what we've always done and keep getting the same results, or do we need to change the way we look at character education, which isn't being provided anywhere else, and begin to teach it ourselves?"

I think the answer is clear.

Teacher

As mentioned in chapter 1, I entered the field of teaching right before NCLB took effect. I felt blessed because, somehow, Florida Atlantic University knew what was coming and molded me into a teach to the test standard-based kind of teacher. I was completely prepared for success. I entered my first classroom with the understanding that my job was to get every single child, no matter how unique, from this point to that point on the standardized test.

In Florida at the time, each elementary school in my district was "awarded" a letter grade based on how the school did on the standardized test. So you would hear comments like, "I teach at an 'A' school" or "I teach at an 'F' school." If a child went to an F school, parents had the option to move their child to an A school, and the district would have to provide transportation for that child. Now, I was lucky enough to teach at an A school, which meant that some of my students rode a bus for 45 minutes or more to come to class. That also meant that these students' parents had to make a 45-minute drive to attend school functions or parent-teacher conferences. Do I really need to tell you how often I saw those parents?

Because I taught in an A school, I also received a pretty hefty bonus each year when our test scores came back. I remember thinking to myself, "Why are we getting a bonus? Why don't they take this money, give it to an F school, and see how it can help?" But I took the money and kept my mouth shut, just like everyone else—and when I say everyone, I mean everyone. I remember attending a staff meeting in which the sole purpose was figuring out how to divvy up the bonus money amongst our staff. Was it just going to go to the teachers? Would the custodians and lunch staff get a cut? After all, they play an important role in the child's education as well. What about the paraprofessionals and school nurses? Administrative assistants? The principal? Now, I don't remember exactly what we decided that day, but I do know that it was quite the debate and there were a lot of hurt feelings by the end of the meeting. I also remember thinking, "I would hate to be the principal right now and have to decide this ridiculous question."

With this public grading system ("public" meaning printed and published in the newspaper for all to see) came tremendous pressure on teachers to make the grade. So, naturally, I taught to the test, shoved away the fun, and drilled and killed. When the students didn't get it, we drilled and killed again. The saddest part about this was that I liked it. I went to work, created well-thought-out lessons, presented them to my class, allowed them time to practice, and then assessed. Those that didn't make the grade, which I considered passing (C or above), were pulled aside and taught/assessed again. I was well trained for this job. There was only one problem: When teaching these lessons, I forgot to look up. I was a robot, teaching these very scripted, standard-based lessons, and I forgot to look up to see if anyone was lost, interested, or maybe even excited about the material. I just plowed through. I had to. The test was coming. The test was coming.

I'm not sure when I decided to actually look up, but I do know that the day I did it stopped me dead in my tracks. What was I doing? What had I become? Who was I teaching? When was the last time I had laughed with my students? Enough! It wasn't working this way. My test scores were high, my school was a success, I was soaring through my standards, and yet none of it was working for me. Academically, I knew each and every one of my students, but socially and personally, I didn't have a clue. I knew absolutely nothing about these kids as individuals. Even worse, they knew nothing about me. I had done an awesome job at preparing these kids for a single test and for the next grade, but I had given them nothing to prepare them for the real test called life.

Why? Mostly because that was how I was trained. I was also in the public eye, and my performance as a teacher was judged by a single test score. Finally, it was financially rewarding to teach in this way.

But what had gotten lost was the reason I got into teaching in the first place. I originally wanted to be with kids and learn alongside them, instead of just standing in the front of a classroom, drilling them on fundamentals. The system just wasn't working for the way I wanted to teach. Change was needed . . . a big change . . . and it had to start with me. It wouldn't be easy. It would mean going up against a lot of powerful people and the general public, but it had to be done. I did not want to teach to the test any longer. I wanted to teach children, individual children, and I wanted to teach the whole child, not just their brains. I wanted to prepare them not for their next academic year, but for life. I simply wanted to teach.

CHAPTER 4

What We've Found

Counselor

To get my counseling credential, I had to complete 600 supervised hours in a school setting. I was lucky enough to land a 28-hour-per-week job with Rosedale, a wonderful elementary school in Chico, California. Even better, it was a paying job, which is rare.

At the end of my first year, I wandered into the library to talk to some of the teachers who had become friends. They were sitting around with file folders, and I noticed that each file had one colored sticker on it: green, yellow, or red.

I asked my buddy what was going on and he told me that it was "next year's draft." The teachers were in the process of picking their students for the following year, and they all wanted to get about the same number of greens (80%), yellows (15%), and reds (5%) in each class, at every grade level.

I asked him what the stickers meant, and he told me that "greens can handle the classroom expectations, yellows struggle from time to time, and reds are the real behavior problems." Most of the reds were kids I worked with during the year, and who had made real progress. Now these students were being labeled based on their behavior in the classroom, and these labels almost certainly affected the teacher's opinion of the child.

In that moment, I realized that we were treating the child, not their lack of social skills and character, as the problem. We were labeling the child, not the behaviors that interfered with his or her ability to co-exist in the classroom, as flawed. To make matters worse, very little was being done to help these students, with the exception of a 30-minute meeting with me once a week.

Almost all the students I worked with loved to come to our meetings. It was a chance for them to get out of class, and they really enjoyed the personal attention of a caring adult. We would talk for a few minutes about the things they struggled with that week, and then we would play a game or shoot some baskets. I doubted that I was making any real progress with the kids and their issues, a fact that I discussed at length with my supervisor. She reassured me that it was enough to just make contact. She also explained how difficult it is to help young children get in touch with their feelings and problems, even if you see them only a few hours after an emotional event. I remember my supervisor telling me, "Kids don't think like adults do. Once they're out of the moment it's gone, and they've moved on." That gave me an idea: If I was going to help them develop new ways of dealing with their issues, I had to be there when the issue came up.

I started going out to recess and watching the kids I worked with as they interacted with others. When I saw them getting upset or about to have a problem, I would immediately go over and talk about what was happening. The difference was amazing. When I got them in the moment, we could talk about how their body was feeling, or what they were thinking at that time. It didn't take long to see results on the playground. It just took the right focus and a short intervention based on a skill, and they began to make some positive changes.

If the problem was significant enough to require more than a quick talk, I'd give the child a time-out to cool off. Then, I'd get back to him or her very quickly, and we would discuss what could have been done differently. If possible, I would have the student re-create the event with the other kid, apologize, and take responsibility for what had occurred.

What I noticed from other adults and playground personnel was that they would just scold the child and hand out a punishment of some sort. Nothing was being done to teach the child a new way to deal with the problem. The kid was labeled as "bad" and told to straighten up and do the right thing. If they don't know what the right thing is, though, how can we expect that student to learn from being punished and told that he or she is bad?

Current parenting and child development research talks extensively about the importance of labeling the action instead of the child. For example, if a kid jumps off the roof, you don't say, "Johnnie, you're an idiot." Instead, you say, "Johnnie, that was an idiotic thing to do." The knife cuts both ways. We also don't want to tell a kid that he or she is smart; instead, compliment the child for working hard. We praise or correct the behavior that created the outcome as opposed to praising or correcting the individual. Why is this so important? It's important because we want those in our care to continually grow, learn, and make better choices. In short, we want life-long learners.

The kid who is labeled as smart can find it very hard to deal with a subject that doesn't come easily, and may take fewer risks. The child that's labeled as angry or stupid can easily assume these roles, and may use them as excuses for not gaining new skills or trying to change behaviors that are not working. People don't really change but behavior can, especially if the new behavior creates real benefits for the person.

I'm the same person I've always been but the behaviors that influence my life are not the same as they were 10, five, or even one year ago. Johnnie is not a bad kid, but his behaviors are creating problems for him in the classroom. He may have developed these negative coping strategies to deal with the dysfunction in his environment. We can continue to label Johnnie as bad and punish him for doing what he's been taught to do, or we can begin to teach him new skills that will work more effectively in the outside world.

My brother is an officer in the Marines, and the Marines are the best I've ever seen at dealing with dysfunctional behavior. They constantly remind the soldiers of what the expectations are, show them what it looks like, and then they drill them (again and again and again) on the proper course of action. They do it to the point that, even in the most stressful situations, soldiers will instinctively turn to their training. They will then respond in the way that is most beneficial to the unit (and the mission), and that may also save their lives. That's the key: Marines know that the person pushing them so hard is trying to give them information that could save their life. There is a very strong bond created between the noncommissioned officers and the recruits, based on survival and necessity. Most organizations don't go to these lengths to train and re-train people.

My uncle once ran the human resources department for a large multinational corporation. He told me that when they were thinking about hiring an individual, they would put him or her through a series of tests to help identify the primary coping strategy of the individual under stress. If the applicant had a particularly negative approach to dealing with stress, the company wouldn't hire that person. This organization understood that making significant changes in his or her behavior would require direct and constant intervention, and it just wasn't worth it.

What that said to me is that for most of us, our primary coping strategies are developed on the playgrounds of elementary schools. We need to help teach these social skills not only so students can function in class, but also in life. When I think back on my own life experience, I realize that anger was my primary coping strategy. I was frequently informed that I had a temper, and I would just have to deal with. That gave me an excuse; it wasn't my fault. It was just something that people would have to learn how to deal with if they wanted to be a part of my life. Guess what? Very few people took me up on that offer.

In truth, I wasn't an angry person; I was a scared and selfish person who thought the world was black or white. I was a person who didn't like to be challenged on my behavior or told what to do. No one taught me how to deal with my selfishness and fear, they just told me I had a temper. Most people in my life tried to punish my temper out of me, and that didn't help. I came to realize that I was angrier with myself than I ever was with another human being. Guilt and self-doubt drove most of my anger. So, punishment was simply an acknowledgement that all the negative thoughts I was thinking about myself were true.

My mom tried to love it out of me. She died in 2005, and I've often said that she gave birth to me for a second time on that day. When she passed, so did my excuses. No matter what I did, or how badly I'd dealt with a situation, Mom could always find a way to make it, at least partly, the other person's fault. She didn't know how to help me either, and she just wanted me to be happy.

Punishment wasn't working, and neither was love. I needed skills. When I finally found my way into a program where I could begin to acquire some skills, my life began to shift. I have seen my behaviors change for the better in this way, not as a result of being threatened or punished. I'm not here to tell you I'm a shining example of these skills in action. I'm closer to where I want to be, yet still deal with issues of selfishness, laziness, and willpower.

Actually, that's why I'm writing this book. I'm still struggling with some of these early coping strategies I picked up along the way. I've had a nicotine habit since I was thirteen years old, and I have struggled with other substances at different times. I don't tell you this to clear my conscience. I tell you this because I believe it's very important to teach these skills early and often, so that the next generation can do a better job than I did in dealing with their deficiencies

For us to make real progress in the area of character development, we need to get out of the labeling and excuse-making business. We can't punish these deficits into extinction as we tried to do with the ruler and the paddle. Nor can we love these kids into making good choices as taught by the failed self-esteem movement of the last 20 years. What we can do is get into the business of teaching kids how we want them to behave, give them constant reminders of what positive character is, and model what it looks like.

This process begins when we identify social-skill problems as a deficiency that can be fixed instead of a personality flaw that is inherited. It might seem obvious to think about heredity, because we can see how closely children mirror their parents in dealing with the world. We have to constantly remind ourselves, however, that this is a learned behavior that can be unlearned if, and only if, we commit to an educational environment that's about relationships first and that actually teaches students how to behave differently.

Teacher

When I moved from Montana to Florida, I had many long hours during the drive to think about this system we call "life in the classroom." I knew what the laws and politicians said, but I also knew that they didn't have it all figured out. The educational pendulum was shifting to focus more on academics, but I wanted to find a way to give equal attention to the development of character traits, too. We have all heard the phrase, "You can't win their heads without first winning their hearts." I knew that I would never be able to truly teach children, to help them reach their true potential, until I got them to trust me with 180 days of their lives.

Upon reflection, I realized that direct character education was the missing piece in my teaching style. I spent the entire summer devising a plan to incorporate what I considered to be the six basic traits of character: respect, responsibility, kindness, citizenship, fairness, and trustworthiness. I needed to find a way to teach those traits to my students, and help those kids develop them as building blocks for their future lives.

My first attempt at this direct character instruction was to isolate each trait during what I called "Character Camp," a two-week program starting on the first day of school. The camp revolved around academic skills such as poetry, literature, songs, art, writing assignments, and daily reflections. All the academics had character traits weaved into them. I was amazed at the tone that the camp set for my classroom. I had always heard about a risk-free classroom, but had not actually seen one in action until this point in my career. The students bonded with each other, and, more importantly, I spent the first two weeks bonding with each child as well. I discovered, through conversations, discussions, and journal writing, the true nature of my students. I discovered how best to meet their individual needs and their unique interests. I learned more about my students in these two weeks than during all my years in Florida combined. While still doing some basic academics (which doesn't really start until week three anyway), I made a student-teacher connection with every single one of my students. I created my own risk-free environment.

Then the camp ended, and it was time to get down to business. When my students would have issues with a specific trait, I would revisit the camp's activities by saying, "Remember when we did this or that activity for that trait during camp?" That helped, but the learning, growing, and connecting had stopped. I was very proud of my progress that year, but I knew that something was still missing.

In phase two of my character plan, I decided not to single out the individual traits, but rather mention them every day. I did this in a small character-circle setting. The inspiration came from an experience in college, when I worked at a small, family-owned Italian restaurant. Before the restaurant opened each day, the staff would have a team meeting in which we talked about the nightly specials, sampled some food, and learned about a new product that we were going to push throughout that evening. It created a sense of unity among the staff. I wanted to apply that to my classroom. Each morning my students would gather around me and we would go over our game plan for the day (the schedule, special events, specialists, etc.). I generally had a poem or a short story that brought out a specific character trait that we would read about and discuss at length. Again, I bonded with the students during this time as personal stories and connections to the texts we were reading came out. I tried very hard to share experiences from my life as well, something with which I was not especially comfortable. I was still struggling with the concept that I was the teacher and they were the students. I feared that if I got personal by sharing my life stories with them, I would become their friend instead of their teacher. But I began to get better at opening up to my students. I also started to notice one more difference: I found myself laughing a lot more, and I mean really laughing out loud. It felt great!

In this phase I also went after the parents. Allow me to preface this part of the story with a little insight into my past history in dealing with parents as an educator. In Florida, I mentioned that most of my students had to travel a great distance to come to school. Therefore, it was almost impossible to get parents to come to the school for a conference or an open house. In my first year as a teacher, I was so excited to talk to ALL the parents about ALL the wonderful things I was going to do. I had even made a PowerPoint presentation! I had more than 30 kids in my class that year; three parents showed up. I was crushed.

As the year progressed and the inevitable disciplinary problems arose, I tried to involve parents in the process. This caused me to run into walls with parents who obviously had negative experiences with school in their own lives. I got the impression that they didn't want to be bothered with school issues; they just wanted me to handle it on my own. My decision was to create an after-school detention program where students literally sat on a chair and stared at a wall for 30 minutes. This punished the student, and it punished their parents because the students then missed the bus ride home. But it also punished me. I now had kids in my classroom after school, during my prep time. I also had to wait for students to get picked up, and I had to see some very angry faces from some very angry parents before I went home for the day. Eventually, I gave up on the parent route and started to handle discipline on my own, during school hours.

Knowing all this, one might begin to understand why I became a little gun-shy and defensive when it came to parental critiques on my teaching style. I decided to take an independent work class called "Getting Parents On Your Side," which offered many common-sense practices and was pretty much a review of tactics I had learned in college. However, the class also presented a new idea: The importance of the bridge between the home and the classroom. I wanted to create a bond between these two key places in the life of the child, and I needed to start even before the beginning of the school year.

So, I began to reach out to the parents personally. I sent out postcards with my picture on them, introducing myself to the families before school started. I contacted each home and shared with them how excited I was about the upcoming school year. I hung out at little league parks and watched baseball games played by former students, hoping to meet upcoming kids (and their parents). In doing all of this, I created an environment that gave the parents a sense of equality. I was not going to judge or intimidate them. My purpose was to mold and change one of the most precious beings in their worlds, and I wanted them to know that I couldn't do it without their help. I wish I could say that I won over every parent that year, but I can't. I too was learning and changing. I did, however, have parents in the classroom more that year than any other year of my teaching career, and my formerly defensive attitude toward parents changed to one in which I learned to listen, empathize, and breathe deeply before responding. All were positive changes, but yet it was still not quite enough.

Phase three of my character integration plan took a strange twist. I became involved with a group at school called TILT, which is a class that teaches teachers how to integrate technology into their classrooms. With that, I was introduced to the concept of blogging. This was truly the missing piece to my home-school bridge. I created a classroom blog and posted to it daily, covering upcoming events in the classroom and in the school. I posted pictures and videos of my students in action. I included their daily assignments and spelling words. All this helped bring the school day into the home setting. Now, when parents would ask their children what they did in school on that day, and received the standard "nothing" answer, those parents could simply read the blog and have a high-quality dinner table discussion with their child. It also eliminated the surprise of projects that were due or upcoming. The blog worked so well that I eventually titled it "A Fly on The Wall." That is exactly what it is; it allows parents to be a fly on the wall of their child's classroom.

As technology helped me bridge the space between the classroom and the home and gain better parental support, I began to expand my character education program to include the digital world as well. I found short YouTube clips of real people showing real character. I dug up sports clips, animal stories, current events, and so on, all of which we watched and then discussed during our Character Circle meetings.

Around this time, I also found Rusty at SchoolToolsTV. I was surfing the Internet one Saturday, trying to find a daily message about character. My students were hearing the messages from me over and over again during our Character Circle, but I wanted them to hear it from others as well. I will never forget the day that I ran across Rusty's site. I was sitting in a coffee shop, and I was so excited that I started clapping out loud. Rusty's message was literally the missing link. In one minute a day, he said everything I wanted to say! I started basing my Character Circle agenda around his topics of discussion. Amazing! The difference this year was I was seeing character really click in a very real way. I was giving them tools and high-interest models of what the traits looked like in the real world . . . in their world.

The final stage, and I hate to use the word "final" here because I know it will be an ever-changing system, was the real Character Circle meetings. My sister, a teacher in North Carolina, introduced me to a book titled *The Morning Meeting Book* by Roxann Kriete.[2] I read it over the summer, and instantly bought into it. I had always done a "morning meeting," but never like this. If you have never read this book, I strongly suggest you purchase it as soon as you finish reading this one. Basically, the meeting is divided into four parts: Morning Greeting, Sharing, Group Activity, and Morning Message. My two absolute favorites are the Morning Greeting and Sharing. In upcoming chapters I will talk more about the different parts of this book and how I implement them into my Character Circle. For now, I just want to share that this style of my Character Circle not only sets the tone for the entire day, but its main focus is to create a sense of unity among the students and a strong, genuine connection with the teacher.

When looking back over these past eight years in Montana, I am amazed at the growth in myself and in my students. I could not have just jumped directly into the stage where I am now. It is a process that had to be taken just a little bit at a time. I often see teachers trying to duplicate my classroom setup, and they become frustrated very quickly. Teaching a character-driven classroom, every single day, is tough! It takes tons of planning, administration support, and, yes, extra work. (Which takes time that none of us has.) But if you start small, by making one small change each year, eventually it all comes together. Even better, it begins to come naturally. I call my teaching model "Grassroots." I just believe that when I teach in this way, I reach the grassroots of the child, and I can see the growth a lot clearer throughout the year. I always tell my class that when they walk out of my classroom at the end of the year, my hope is that they take with them all they have learned academically, but even more important, I want them to take the social skills and the power to believe in themselves and others. Those are the skills that will truly help them succeed in the real world.

Developing strong, positive character traits takes years and years of practice, and it is imperative that we give our students those tools, in addition to the necessary academics. The skills to figure out an academic problem and the ones needed to determine the proper character-based course of action are different. Students have to grow into their character, and it has to be modeled and experienced over time for them. This takes discussions, patience, grace, and forgiveness on our part. It takes listening, willingness, tears, and hugs on theirs. The best part is that we can do this; we can actually mold a human being into one of strong character, one that is ready to tackle the world with his or her head held high. We can help them steer clear of bullies, drugs, alcohol, gangs, and other dangerous distractions. By giving them the tools they need to stand up for themselves right now, we can look into the past and the future with pride. It is our job to make a difference in the lives of children. This is one sure way of doing just that.

CHAPTER 5

Making a Difference

Counselor

> "Good teaching cannot be reduced to technique; good teaching comes from the identity and integrity of the teacher."
>
> —Parker J. Palmer,
> *The Courage to Teach: Exploring*
> *the Inner Landscape of a Teacher's Life*[3]

"To thine own self be true." The teacher who first brought this idea to my awareness was Rose Threlkeld, or as I called her, "Mrs. T." Mrs. T taught English at London Central High School in England, which I attended from 1978 until I graduated in 1981. LCHS was a dorm school for most of us, and the kids from my base stayed there four or five nights a week. This was the perfect environment for self-discovery. I was away from my parents most of the time, which required becoming more self-reliant. It also provided me with more opportunity for introspection than a normal high school; I remember that the weather in England played a major role in this as well.

It rained or was overcast for most of the three years I spent on that island nation. At the time, the fashion for people like me was to wear a hooded sweat shirt under my jock jacket, and to keep the hood on between classes or while walking around campus after school let out. I find it interesting that most of the kids I work with today wear the same kind of uniform, and we constant have to remind them to take their hoods off. Maybe, as was the case with me, they're both hiding from a world that's uncontrollable while beginning to notice and make sense of their inner voice. I can see why monks wear hoods, as it really does foster a sense of being alone, both in the world and with one's thoughts. This helps bring the inner dialogue more clearly into focus. I call it a dialogue but it was much more like a battle between conflicting voices trying to control who I was and who I was going to be. Mrs. T first introduced me to others who had fought similar kinds of battles in the past.

I was in her English composition class my junior year. Although I did OK in her class, I never thought of Mrs. T as a mentor or even as someone who had taken an interest in me. That all changed the day she came into the library while I was filling out my senior schedule. She walked directly to my table, took the sheet out of my hand, and wrote in "Honors Shakespeare" as one of my electives. I had completed almost all of the classes I needed to graduate and had only two core classes remaining. That meant I could load up on electives. My plan was to take the easiest load possible, and to focus on sports and other extra-curricular activities like chasing the girl who had been the object of my affection for more than a year. I had no desire to take Mrs. T's class, and I told her so. She simply looked at me and said, "I'll expect you in my class next fall," and walked away. For some reason, I didn't erase what she had written, and that was one of the best decisions I've ever made.

The class opened my eyes for many reasons, not the least of which was that she taught the class with records from the Royal Shakespeare Company. I soon discovered that I'm an audio learner, and that I have a gift for memorization. This helped me immensely going forward in my education because, as we all know, memorization is the backbone of our educational system (or should I say, training system.) Even more than that, I connected with the subjects of those great plays, and the way Mrs. T brought their inner battles to life. I understood Hamlet and his self-doubt, Othello's jealousy, the ambitions of Macbeth, and many of the love-struck characters in the comedies. Most of all, I identified with Prince Hal, who went on to become the great King Henry V, a man still revered for his successful reign. Shakespeare's play was highlighted by Henry's victorious campaign against France, culminating with the famous Battle of Agincourt.

It didn't start out that way for Hal. He had a reputation for being a spoiled, lazy brat who spent more time goofing off than in pursuit of "kingly" aspirations. Most people, especially his father, thought he was destined to be an underachiever all his life. He turned it around by using what he had learned from his time spent with the "common" folks (most of whom he'd met in pubs) and became a great king who married a princess and led his country to greatness.

I first met Prince Hal in Henry IV Part 1 and 2, and connected with him immediately. To me, he was a struggling young man trying to find himself. He had friends in low places, enjoyed having a good time, and had some persistent doubts about how it was all going to work out. But he also had a belief in himself that no one could shake. Prince Hal believed he was going to overcome all the self-imposed obstacles in his way and fulfill his destiny. Soliloquies were Shakespeare's way of letting us hear his characters' inner voices, and Mrs. T made us memorize one from each play. To this day, I still recite Hal's words because they remind me that I, too, will find my way and make the most of what I've been given.

When the year was over, I asked Mrs. T to sign my yearbook. She wrote one simple quote and nothing more: "To thine own self be true." At the time, I was a little disappointed, having thought she would go on and on about what a great kid I was. I wondered if maybe I was just another student to her. However, I've come to realize that she gave me the greatest challenge any mentor could offer a protégé; it was a road map to a life based on fulfillment and purpose. You don't offer that kind of challenge to someone you don't truly believe in. Much later, as she was dealing with terminal cancer, I would learn through a letter from her that my intuition had been correct: I wasn't just another student to Mrs. T. She saw something special in me, and she had never stopped talking about how she knew I was destined to say something that needed to be heard. Through Hal's soliloquy and several other verses I've picked up over the years, not a day goes by that I don't offer a silent thank-you to Mrs. T. Even though Hal is one of my historical heroes, the teacher who introduced me to him is one of my most important real-life heroes, and the one who helped give context to my journey.

I find it fascinating how life sometimes imitates art. My first long-term job after college was that of a bartender working in Georgetown, a suburb of Washington D.C. My parents were deeply concerned about my lifestyle, and how and when I planned on getting a "real" job. I vividly remember taking my father to Kenneth Branagh's film version of Henry V at a theater around the corner from the bar where I worked. I also remember almost crying my way through the whole thing, as I explained what was going on and how I planned to find my way as well. I'm not sure he really got it, but I'll always appreciate him going with me.

Being true to myself, then as well as now, requires that I continue to learn and grow as a person and as a professional. It requires me to be open to new ideas and ways of doing things. It requires that I live up to another part of my mantra, which is to be true to myself in a world that's trying night and day to make me like everyone else. This is the hardest battle I have to fight, and it's ongoing. It is a daily challenge, one that must be accepted by those who, like me, seek purpose and passion in their lives. This is especially relevant for those of us in education, because our clients can smell insincerity and doubt a mile away. I think the reason that kids connect with my show is because they can tell that I'm not someone who is just saying these things. I believe in what I'm doing, and it's a part of who I am. I'm not saying I'm perfect, or that I get it right even half the time. The show works because I'm talking with them about ideas that are near to my life purpose, ones that inspire me to do better.

As teachers and counselors, our job is not to get students through the year or get them to high school graduation. Our job is to give students the skills and ideas that will help them to take their own journeys inward and find the voices that only they can speak. In the next chapter we will discuss the idea of relationships, and how vital they are to this process. For now, it's important to realize that the most important relationship is the one we have with ourselves. Each of us is an army of one who must rely on our own sense of who we are and what's important to give ourselves more fully to others.

The steps to become more self-aware are as varied as the people who will pick up this book. It's not the how that's important; it's the how often. Here are a few simple things to remember. First, practice silence. It's easy to forget to turn the world off, and that can lead to a life based on white noise. To hear what's going on in your world, turn off the radio in the car or take a walk without headphones. To get a sense of the day, sit in a quiet spot for a few minutes before you go home, and make some mental notes about what worked and what didn't. After you make those mental notes, consider putting them down on paper. Journaling is one of the best ways to keep track of where you are on the path, and is a powerful tool for letting go of frustrations and disappointments.

Finally, and most important, face your fear. I saw a bumper sticker recently that said, "Life begins at the edge of your comfort zone." I'm not a religious man so I have little to say about things so far above my pay grade, but when people ask me if I believe in life after death, I always say that I'm more interested in life after birth, because most of us live in fear, which is the lowest form of human existence. Fear is the mind killer and the destroyer of dreams.

Whatever it is that scares you and holds you back, take it slowly out of the closet. Then, look it squarely in the eye. If it's something that's broke, fix it. If it's something that you can't control or that belongs to someone else, just recognize it for what it is and give it a name. To name something is to know it. Even though most of my thoughts are slow to change, I now recognize them for what they are and they don't get in my way as much as they did before. I've also come up with replacement thoughts that I consciously insert into my mental processes when negativity and fear attempt to take hold.

You may or may not be able to count on the organization you work for or the parents/guardians of the students you teach. If you can count on yourself, however, that will be more than enough to give those kids a fighting chance. In addition, it will give you the kind of satisfaction that only comes with being true to yourself. As we start to become more comfortable with who we are, we can be more open and available for others. I think Haim Ginott said it best: "I've come to the frightening conclusion that I am the decisive element in the classroom. It's my daily mood that makes the weather."[4]

Teacher

Every once in awhile, I find myself reaching a point of total frustration. When this happens I convince myself that I am going to come to work, shut my door, work, open my door, and go home. I refuse to do anything extra, and I teach as if I'm just here to collect a paycheck. Now, this feeling usually comes after a heated conversation with the district powers, administration, or a parent, and luckily only lasts about 24 hours, but it is real nonetheless. There are times when I feel like I am the only one that really gets it; the only one looking out for what is best for the children in my care. I feel like I'm an outsider looking in and saying, "Really . . . ?" I feel like an army of one.

The type of teaching that I have described all along is hard. It is draining at times. It demands you to be human on all sorts of levels. It can make you ask, "Why?" a million times a day: Why do I care? Why do I go above and beyond? Why don't their parents teach this at home? Why won't my principal trust me? Why don't the higher powers in the district understand that kids can't learn to their true potential if they don't have a trusting relationship with me? Why does it take so much time to create a classroom of unity? Why do I love each and every one of these kids as if they were my own? Why, why, why . . .

The type of teaching I have proposed is also one that requires the teacher to reflect daily, if not hourly. All the time, I find myself saying, "I should really practice what I preach," or "I need to work on that in my own life." I am not perfect. I am human. I don't walk around all high and mighty on character. My character is questioned by myself and those around me all the time. You have to understand that when you teach in a character-based model, you will find yourself changing every single day. You will apply everything that you teach to your own life. At times, that is VERY uncomfortable. It is easy to say the right things to kids, but taking action in your own adult life is harder than you can ever imagine. Knowing this in advance and still accepting the challenge is the first step.

As I mentioned before, when I was in school, I don't remember encountering the issues that kids face today. I heard about drugs, alcohol, abuse, and gangs, but I don't remember seeing it in "real" life. Today kids come to school deprived of parental love on a daily basis. They don't receive constant and real attention from the people that are supposed to love them the most. They come to school and say they are sad during the feeling time portion of my character meetings, because their parents were not home to tuck them in or wake them up. They are treated like things instead of human beings. The term "family" had a different meaning for me as a small child than it does for most of my students today. Even though my own parents were divorced when I was very young, I still saw many nuclear families. Now, my kids come to me with no parents, one poor parent, grandparents for parents, or multiple families made up of their friend's parents. My students don't even understand what a mom, dad, sister, brother, and pet-dog-named-Rover family is anymore, because it's just not normal to come from a family like that. Those kids are now foreign in the public schools. I imagine that life as a teacher must have been easier when I was a child. I imagine supportive parents and patient administrators. I imagine all sorts of learning in all of our activities. I imagine fiction.

For decades, teachers have been dealing with various issues that happen outside our classroom walls. The issues might be different, but our actions are the same. We stop what we are doing, and we take the teachable moment to love a child in emotional need. We take charge, and we make executive decisions to give a child a hug or talk with that child within the group or one-on-one. We laugh with them. We cry with them. We build relationships with them. Then . . . they learn. Teachers have known this secret for years.

I remember when I conducted the Character Camp that I described in chapter 4.[5] The local newspaper showed up the day we distributed the homeless kits. It was a very proud moment for me. Then I got online and read some of the comments people submitted about the story. I remember one in particular. The anonymous writer wrote that he or she was appalled that I would waste a week's worth of time doing this "fluff." The letter criticized the fact that I undertook all these activities that had nothing to do with learning. What they didn't understand was that I just saved myself a million minutes of discipline, during precious instruction time, by creating relationships with my students on a personal level. My experience has proven time and time again that if you teach the way I propose to teach, your discipline problems practically vanish overnight, because the students link you with someone that they want to please. They trust you to lead them to the right way of doing things, and to hold them accountable. They want to do right simply because they like you, and they don't want to disappoint you.

One of my students once lied to me about changing an answer on a paper while self-grading it. I pulled the child out into the hall for a one-on-one conversation. I knew the child had done it, and the child knew I knew it, but the lie went so deep that the student didn't know how to tell the truth. When the student finally cracked and broke down into tears, my response was, "I am not mad at you. I am proud of you for telling the truth in the end. However, I am very disappointed in you and your actions to deceive me." The child wept in my arms and promised repeatedly not to do it again. I believed the student and reassured her that I knew that she would make better choices in the beginning next time.

Although my disappointment was the worst punishment for that little girl, at the same time it was the absolute best consequence for her. She never lied to me again. Actually, I had two other instances where I had to become involved with questionable acts concerning her. As soon as I entered into the picture, she automatically retracted any false statement she had made and told the truth immediately. She didn't want to hear the disappoint statement again from me, an adult who had earned her respect and trust by taking the time in the first week of school to show her that I am human just like her.

Many times, I sit in meetings that are designed to form a plan of action for a particular child. Sometimes these are Individualized Education Program (IEP) meetings, and sometimes they are just teachers brainstorming together. In both situations I have found one common phrase being used: "If only the parents would get involved." I have come to discover that this is an extremely hard phrase for teachers to understand and accept. As teachers, we don't understand how an adult who has brought a child into this world would not love him or her just like we do. It seems unforgivable that a parent would not return a phone call, come to a school conference, attend school functions, or even at times provide the basic food, shelter, and love that every child needs to grow up healthy. Sadly, all this occurs, and with greater and greater frequency.

Parents just don't seem to have or want the responsibilities of getting involved with their child's education. As sad as that is, I have decided that I will not expect or question a parent's involvement any longer. There have been two personal consequences for me stemming from this conclusion. First, I find myself less disappointed and more willing to find workable solutions within the school setting. Second, I find that more parents are slowly coming back out of the woodwork. Why? Because the relationship I pursue with them is not one of guilt or blame toward their parenting style, but one of trust and approval for my actions. I am giving them the freedom to seek me out only if they chose to, and that is very powerful. I have always found it difficult to trust unreliable sources. Therefore, I choose not to and welcome the unexpected surprises every once in awhile.

Sometimes in our profession, it's best to just nod your head, go into your classroom, shut the door, and do what you feel is right. This generally happens when we are asked (meaning told) by the powers above that we need to teach in a certain way. We know by now that there is no point in arguing or asking why we have to do whatever it is that they think we need to do. So, we just agree.

I believe that teachers, as the professionals on the spot, are the ones to make the best decisions about how to handle the children in our care. I am not sure how it is in your district, but in mine I often find that the decisions made by the bigwigs at the district level cost a ton of money and are not approved by teachers. These people form committees of teachers and select computer programs and textbooks for the entire district without taking the time to ask each teacher if these tools fit into his or her classroom. Then they demand that we set aside more of our precious instructional time to implement these programs. All the while, the district and the general public complain about how the district has no money to buy the book sets, computer labs, or art supplies that many teachers request. Meanwhile, I have brand-new science books that will be outdated next week sitting on the back shelf of my classroom, and computer programs that require me to stagger my kids in 20-minute intervals all day long. Now, I can get frustrated about this situation, or I can make the choice to just accept it and go about my teaching. I chose to accept this behavior as normal. I could fight it all the way to the top, but why? I have better ways to exert my energy.

There are times, however, when a teacher must stand up to the powers above. Let me give you an example. In our district, our fourth graders were required to take three standardized tests: the MontCas, the NWEA, and the IOWA Basics. All three test virtually the same things: reading comprehension and math skills. So naturally, when I became a fourth-grade teacher, I was very confused as to why my kids were taking the same test three times, and why I was losing more than a month of my instructional teaching time. So, I dared to ask the dreaded "why" question. The answer I got did not surprise me at all: My fourth graders were taking the same test three times because of money granted from different levels of the government. The MontCas is a state test, the NWEA is a local test, and the IOWA Basics test is national. To receive funds from each agency, their specific test has to be given. I did not stop there. I then asked why students couldn't just take one test, the results of which all the agencies would share. Of course this would never fly, but upon further research, it was discovered that the IOWA Basics could be dropped in our district. So now, because one teacher took a stand in the best interest for kids, our fourth graders now only have to take the same test twice instead of three times. It's still confusing, but two tests are better than three. It should be noted here that in this same school year I asked to transfer to a school closer to my home and was denied. The same person that had to do all the research on the tests also makes the transfer decisions. Coincidence? I don't know, but it makes one wonder now, doesn't it? The point that I am trying to make here is that there will be times when a true teacher has to sacrifice his or her own well-being for the sake of the children's best interests. There are times when we cannot shut our doors and nod our heads. There are times when we have to act. It is always worth it in the end, trust me.

An army of one: That is a true statement if you accept the challenge. It does not mean that you will always be all alone. It simply means that there will be times when you will have to make decisions that may or may not align with the norm. You must have the courage to accept that you may have to stand up to some pretty intimidating people, whether it be parents, colleagues, administrators, or the higher district powers. You have to pick your battles, but when it really matters you need to have the guts to stand up for the best outcomes for your students. You, and you alone, can and do make a huge difference, and that is very, very powerful.

CHAPTER 6

Building Trust-Based Relationships

Counselor

My mom used to always say that trust is the basis of any relationship. I've come to realize that, as usual, she was right. Of course, also as usual, I had to learn this lesson the hard way.

I was married to a very nice woman for a brief period of time, but it never really took. I used to say I got married and then I got a dog, and what I realized was all I needed was a dog. I say that jokingly but there's a lot of truth to that statement. I trusted my dog and my dog trusted me. I trusted myself to do what needed to be done to care for my dog, but when it came to my marriage, I wasn't nearly as confident. I was raised with the old story that two people become one in a marriage. I actually believed that married couples shared all the same goals and interests, which was fine with me because I was mainly interested in myself.

I've had the good fortune of watching my brothers and sister enjoy healthy marriages for the last 20-plus years. What I've come to realize is that a good marriage is not two people becoming one, but two people committing to a third entity, the relationship itself. Each person has to trust that the other has the best interest of the relationship in mind and is willing to commit, make sacrifices, and give of themselves to help the relationship grow and prosper. I wasn't able to do this in my relationship, mostly because I wasn't sure who I was or where I was going. I didn't really trust myself because I had gotten so far off track.

I was reminded of that track a few years after my divorce, when I dug up a college paper I had written at the age of 20, in 1983. I wrote it for an English class, and the subject was "Who do you think you are?" What struck me when I read it years later was how closely the words describe the man I am today. Let me say right off the bat that I realize now that this was a part of the road I had to take to get to where I am today, but at that moment (just after the breakup of my marriage) I was filled with a great sense of lost time and dead ends.

In that paper, I wrote about wanting to be a counselor and a coach. However, I had convinced myself that to be happy doing that, I needed money. So after college, I went about buying businesses I knew nothing about, hoping they would bring me the fortune I thought I needed to pursue my dreams.

I started off with network marketing schemes that failed because I couldn't bring myself to force my loved ones into my "downline." Then it was a hotdog cart which I planned to run in Washington D.C. or at the beach where I was a bartender on the weekends. That didn't go well because I had no idea of how firmly entrenched real vendors were to their spots. Therefore, finding a good area to place the stand was an issue with the locals. The best part of that whole experience was that the cart was eventually stolen, which meant I didn't have to find a way to dispose of the thing.

From there I went on to selling recharged laser printer cartridges, which was a great idea, but cold-calling prospects was a bit out of my league. I ended up selling renewable phone cards in San Francisco, which is where my soon-to-be ex-wife entered the scene.

What does all this have to do with trust in a relationship, you ask? You see, when I met my future wife, I had convinced myself that I was a businessman destined to strike it rich in the new California Gold Rush that was the Internet boom of the late '90s. That was the guy who dated and eventually married her.

After we got married, I had some serious doubts about my business plans and I started going off in all kinds of directions, trying to find out who I "really" was. Imagine my wife's disorientation. She would wake up every day to a guy who was totally depressed because he couldn't find his way in the world, and come home to a guy who had a new quick fix about how he was going to make it all work. I wouldn't say I was acting bipolar, but I was definitely the conductor of my own personal roller coaster. She was none too happy to be along for the ride and the relationship suffered. She couldn't trust me. Can you blame her?

Second, I didn't really trust her. There were several important areas where we didn't connect but instead of trusting my intuition and calling it off, I kept going farther. She was this beautiful, talented woman from a great family, so I thought I would be crazy to let those doubts get in the way. Instead of going with my gut, I went down the aisle.

Finally, life got complicated. I got fired from a high-paying job just two weeks before we got married, and I spent the next 18 months struggling to sell my phone cards. My ex, on the other hand, quit a solid job for a commission-only position in sales, which she had never tried before. She turned out to be a rock star in her new role, making more than $150,000 her first full year. That was great for her, but unfortunately my ego was taking a beating.

We had bought a house in San Francisco right before we got married and were in the process of fixing it up. Then we decided to move closer to her family so we had to get the house ready to sell. Now a lot of you might be thinking that these are the normal trials and tribulations of the first few years of marriage, and you'd be right. But try overcoming those trials without trusting your partner.

We sold the house and moved to Austin, Texas, where we hoped that a change of venue could help us rekindle our relationship. Without trust, however, nothing changes and it became clear to both of us that things weren't going to work out, so we decided to go our separate ways. I needed to go somewhere and find myself, but where would I go?

We'd moved to Austin from San Francisco, where my brother and his family still resided. My mom and dad lived in Harpers Ferry, West Virginia, and my sister and her family lived in Northern Virginia. Everyone on my dad's side of the family lived in the Washington, D.C. area, where I had gone to college and had lived for eight years before moving to San Francisco.

As you can see, I had a lot of logical options but none of them really entered my mind. I knew of a small town in northern California named Chico, and it was there that I'd make my new start. At the time, I didn't really know why, but something inside of me realized that at the very least, I needed to start trusting myself again. If things were going to change, it would have to start with me. So I loaded a truck with my dog Jake by my side and I left Austin in pursuit of some answers and a fresh start in a place where no one knew my name.

For the next seven years, Jake and I walked the peaks and valleys of Chico while I asked myself serious questions about all the relationships in my life. The one theme that kept coming back to me over and over again was trust. It became clear to me that my wife didn't trust me nor I her and without that, nothing else really mattered. We weren't focused on that third entity, the relationship itself, and we didn't do the kinds of things that build trust in a relationship. When life got tough, we turned to others for advice and counsel, or reached for negative coping strategies to try and avoid the problems at hand.

What I came to realize was that trust is something that is built, brick by brick, day after day. It's not a given and can't be taken for granted. When it's broken, apologies only go so far, but when the bond is strong, it gives the people in the relationship the courage to take risks and commit more fully to the task at hand. What I also learned was that when it comes to education, it's all about relationships, too.

I recently attended a retreat for a school I worked with in California. A facilitator was brought in to help the teachers "bond" by doing a variety of team-building activities, all of which were meant to create trust amongst the staff.

After it was all over, I found myself among the crowd of participants, who were all sitting in their grade-level groups. What I noticed was that they were talking about how this kind of stuff never works. Most notably, they spoke in very negative ways about the principal, who was conspicuously absent that day.

Their comments ranged from mild to obscene, but they all were saying basically the same thing, which can be summed up with one quote I'll never forget. It came from a veteran teacher who'd taught at the school for 17 years, who said: "He [the principal] is always telling us that we should communicate and work together, but then he goes behind our backs every chance he gets."

What struck me about that quote was how much it reminded me of my failed marriage. At that moment, I realized that it's one thing to talk a good game but it's a whole other thing to live these values on a daily basis as we go about our business. Without trust in a marriage, partners have no reason to go deeper and grow. Without trust in the leadership of a school or an organization, the staff will only do the bare minimum to get by. Without trust in the teacher in the classroom, the students won't take risks and push themselves to new levels.

If we say one thing and do another, will they trust us? If we're not consistent and aware of how we affect the climate of our own classroom, will they trust us? If we aren't willing to commit to creating that third entity, the relationship, with each of the students we're responsible for, will they trust us enough to do the things we need them to do? All relationships are based on trust, and effective education is all about building relationships. Mom, you were right as usual.

Teacher

Building relationships with students takes a tremendous amount of commitment. I have shared in the past few chapters some of the obstacles that you will need to overcome to create relationships with students. Now, I will share with you how I do it in my classroom.

It actually starts before the students even arrive on the first day. I send a postcard to their homes, with my picture on it. (Lifetouch school photos makes them.) I tell them a little bit about myself and how happy I am that they are in my class. I then shock them with a sentence directly about them. What they don't know is that I go to the previous year's teacher and ask for a strength or interest for each student. I then make a connection with the child. For example, little Johnny might like baseball. So, I might write a phrase like this: "Johnny, you and I have something in common: I am a huge baseball fan. I love to take my two children to the Billings Mustangs games. I also played softball when I was your age and even made the All-Star team once." This is the first step in building a relationship with Johnny. He now has something to talk to me about on the first day of school. I have also just told him that I am a real human being with a life just like his. We all know that kids believe we do nothing but teach at their schools. If you don't believe me, then just go hang out at the local Walmart and see the terrified look on students' faces when they see you, their teacher, in public, wearing casual clothing. Or, really shock them and show up at one of their sporting events in sweats and a baseball cap. They just don't think we are real; they believe we are robots who live and sleep at school.

Next comes the first day. I take the time in the morning, before the first bell rings, to go out and meet each student as they arrive at school. I shake their hand, I look them in the eyes, and I introduce myself to them. I know who they are because I spent the week before studying the previous year's yearbook pictures, so I already know what they look like and their names. I also get to meet a lot of the parents during this time.

Our district generally starts school on a Wednesday. Therefore, the first week of school is only three days long. I spend those three days building routines, procedures, and unity. The first thing my class does, on day one, is to have our character meeting. I have referenced this idea earlier but now I want to talk about it in more depth. Let me begin by saying this is my very favorite part of the school day.

In the first week, we spend a lot of time studying the concepts of shaking hands with others, making good eye contact, and what it means to be an American. Let's start with the handshake. I pose the question, "When and how did handshakes start?" We brainstorm answers and then we turn to the computer. Through the research, we discover that the history of handshakes is not set in stone. The kids' favorite theory is that knights used to shake hands all the way up to their elbows. This was not to be friendly, but was to check for weapons hidden up someone else's sleeves. Have them try it. We then go over the etiquette of handshaking. There are specific rules for boys, girls, men, and women when it comes to shaking hands with each other. Then we practice it. You can help kids build their confidence by asking them to shake hands with staff members. One thing I have noticed is that kids often lack the ability to look adults in the eye when greeting them. Expect this at first, but encourage them to look up at you when they greet you every morning.

Next, we look at the American citizen concept. During our character meeting, we dissect the pledge of allegiance. There are some really good online resources on how to do this. We watch numerous YouTube videos showing soldiers fighting for our rights. We talk a lot about what public education means and how students must never take it for granted. We also watch some videos on children in the Middle East that do not have the same educational opportunities as students in this country. Comparing and contrasting these experiences is always an eye-opener for my fourth graders. Kids need to understand that education has not always been the same in America. It has come a long way, and they are lucky enough to live in a time where education is free and open for everyone. It's also great to read about the history of the flag, our current president, and the meaning of America. You will be amazed at the generalizations and misconceptions that come from these discussions. Other concepts, such as war, racism, and women's rights, lead to some very strong and sometimes shocking statements from the children, which often come directly from the home. Be prepared to address these issues, and be ready for follow-up discussions with some parents as well.

The best way to cement the student-teacher relationship is during feelings time. This is done at my character meeting, and takes about 10 to 15 minutes each day. This is where I go around the circle and ask each child how he or she is feeling on that day. They have a feeling poster in their journal with all the different feeling faces that can help guide them. At first, they will usually say, "Happy" or "Sad." Eventually, though, they will become more specific in their feelings. For example, by the end of this past year, my class described feelings such as "hilarious," "mischievous," "frantic," and "guilty."

Each child is required to say how they are feeling and why. No one is allowed to comment on anyone else's feelings due to time restraints. As the teacher, I must acknowledge their feelings and respond back to validate them. For example, little Suzie might say that she is feeling sad today because her grandma is in the hospital. I would reply, "I am sorry to hear that you are sad today. It is always scary to have a loved one in the hospital." I might go on to question why grandma is in the hospital. I would end by commenting that I will be thinking of her and her grandma throughout the day. The next day, and this is very important to this process, I make sure to ask Suzie how her grandma is doing. I want her to know that I remembered what she said and that her feelings and home life are important to me. I also have another opportunity to make a connection here. Often, when I hear of family happenings that are sad or happy, I will e-mail the parent as well. In this case, I might e-mail Suzie's mom, saying that she shared during feelings time that she was sad and worried about her grandma. I would express to the parent that I am thinking of all of them and to let me know if I can help in any way. All of this creates a bond between the child and me, and sometimes with their families as well. I always end feelings time by saying how I am feeling. It is important for them to understand that I have feelings as well. It creates a sense of empathy in them.

Every day I end the character meeting with a call and response. I, the teacher, say: "You are very important to me!" (I say this VERY slowly while making eye contact with each and every student.) They respond back to me with: "I am an amazing person even when I make a mistake, and I will do my very best to learn and grow from it. I BELIEVE in me!" It is important to note that many times I chime in with them and say this as well. It allows them to see that I, too, make mistakes and learn and grow from them every day.

Lastly, I also build relationships with my students when they are absent from school. Directly after the morning meeting, my students spend about 15 minutes getting ready for their day. During this time I am e-mailing parents. When a child is absent I try very hard to send their parents an e-mail, which would read something like this: "Dear Mr. and Mrs. Smith, I noticed that your daughter Sally is not in class today. I hope that everything is OK. Please tell Sally that I miss her, and that class is just not the same without her. Let her know that I hope I see her later today or tomorrow morning. If there is anything I can do to help please let me know. Take care."

Creating relationships with children builds trust. Trust comes to children through love. Parents are a child's first experience of the love-equals-trust factor. Understanding that a teacher is the closest thing to a child's parents can be frightening. It takes a special type of teacher to create a lasting relationship with a child. Once you have a relationship built upon trust you can move to the next level, which is teaching them to believe in themselves. That, however, is another chapter in itself.

CHAPTER 7

Respect

Counselor

In 2005, I got my first head coaching job in basketball, working with seventh-grade girls. I was excited about the prospect of teaching them everything there was to know about the game, so I found a website by a seasoned coach that listed all the skills a good team needed to master to be successful. The list had 30 or 40 items on it. As I looked it over, I started to get worried about fitting all of these things into a pair of hour-long practices each week. I prepared a detailed plan for each practice and spent the entire hour running around yelling at the kids, who were totally confused and frustrated, as I tried to rush them through all the drills and ideas I was trying to teach.

At the end of one practice, the coach whose team was using the gym after us came up to me and said, "You really have a lot going on our there. What are you trying to teach them?" I told him about the website and even showed him a print-out of the skills list I'd found. He looked at the list and then he gave me some of the best advice I've ever received. He said, "Pick three or four things from this list and get really good at those. The rest will take care of itself."

Becoming good at a very few things has been my motto ever since. Professionally, I focus on SchoolToolsTV, my coaching practice, and my basketball club. As a basketball coach, I focus on man-to-man defense, fundamentals, and the read-and-react offense. Personally, I focus on self-awareness, relationships, and balance.

When it comes to teaching social skills, I faced a similar dilemma because social skills are defined as anything that facilitates interaction and communication with others, from simple facial expressions to complex bonding rituals. After extensive research and experience working with kids, I realized that my efforts were best spent helping them develop the ability to interact with others and to function in groups. The three skills that they needed to succeed were respect, responsibility, and resiliency, or as I like to call them, "The Other Three Rs." This chapter is about developing self-respect; we'll discuss responsibility and resiliency in chapters 8 and 9, respectively.

Respect for oneself is the cornerstone of any effort to create an empathic individual, and is also a prerequisite for the development of responsibility and resiliency. The ability to understand your own worth allows for a greater openness and acceptance of others. A sense of individual purpose leads to responsibility for one's actions and protects against becoming a victim of circumstance. The ability to deal with mistakes and failure and an appreciation for one's unique strengths and weaknesses creates a willingness to never give up, even in the face of the most challenging situations.

The concept of self-respect is not new. In fact, for the last 30 years, educational gurus have been telling teachers and parents that the way to boost children's sense of self-respect is to lavish praise on them. The self-esteem movement's mantra was, "You can be whatever you want to be." Its emblem was the participation award that all children received, regardless of whether or not they had excelled or even tried in any given activity.

I'll illustrate this with a story. I once walked into a classroom and found a teacher frantically searching the Internet. I asked her what she was looking for and she said she needed one more award for a student. I asked her what the award was for and she said, "That's the problem. The student hasn't really done anything all year but I was told by the principal that every child had to receive at least one award at the promotion ceremony." She went on to tell me that the child had Cs and Ds in every subject, not because he wasn't smart, but because he refused to do any work and that he'd been absent more than 50 times. The child had numerous referrals for bullying and aggressive behavior, had been suspended several times, and had even cursed her out earlier in the year. Two things came to mind as I was driving away from her classroom. First, we must be stupid if we think that kids don't see right through fake compliments and gestures. Second, what does rewarding this kind of behavior, even if it is only a token reward, say to the kids who really tried?

The reason I'm good at what I do is because kids trust me. I speak to them as I speak with any other real people, and I tell them what I think. I'm honest with them and they appreciate it to the point that it even translates well over the Internet.

Most children are incredibly intuitive and though they may not understand the nuances of a situation, they can tell the difference between right and wrong, truth and lie, sincere and phony better than most adults I know. The process of teaching children how to respect themselves starts with being honest and treating them like individuals. As a public speaker, I'm very aware of what's called the "verbal crutch," which is the annoying habit of a speaker using a particular word or phrase, like "um" or "you know," over and over during a presentation. One of the things I've notice with adults is that they often have a word or a phrase that they use repeatedly with all children, like "sweetie" or "big boy." I once worked with a woman who called all of her kids "rockin'" or "rock star," as in, "There's rockin' Rusty" or "Rusty, you're a rock star." I talked to her about it one day but it fell on deaf ears, and she continued to do it even when a kid got in trouble and had to be reprimanded. She would say something like, "Hey rockin' Rusty, I need you to get back on track and start doing your work like the rock star I know you are." I was often there when this was going on and sometimes the kid would look at me after the teacher turned away, as if to say, "Is she serious?"

One of the best ways to really connect with kids and show them that you see their individuality is to give them a nickname. It shouldn't be something obvious or a silly rhyme, but one that's unique or reflects some shared experience.

Earlier, I told you about Coach Wise and the effect he had on me. He gave me one of the greatest nicknames I ever had. He called me "RD," for "Rusty Dog." Now, that may not sound too attractive to you, but it meant the world to me. The year I got my "RD" nickname, we had several good running backs on our team, and I was the fullback. For those of you who are not familiar with football, the fullback is really a glorified guard, whose job it is to line up in the backfield and block so that the running back can get free and score.

I was also the outside linebacker, and I just loved to hit people. It didn't matter to me whether or not I got the tackle just as long as I hit a few blockers and forced the play into other defenders who got credit for the tackle. During a game early in our ninth-grade season, I intercepted a pass and was running in the direction of three players from the other team, who were about 10 yards away.

Instead of doing the smart thing and trying to run around them, I went directly at the biggest of the three, put my head down, and tried to run him over. He outweighed me by about 50 pounds but he must have lost his balance because he went flying backwards while the other two players wrapped me up. The big guy was none too happy about what had happened and we got into a fight on the field.

Coach Wise came running off the sideline and literally dragged me back to the bench before things got out of hand. He went back to coaching the game and gave me a few minutes to calm down before he returned and said: "That's one of the dumbest things I've ever seen and one of the bravest. You're always doing the dirty work, Mr. May. I think I'll call you Rusty Dog from now on." He then walked away. Good thing he did, or else he would have seen the tears of pride well up in my eyes.

If you can connect with kids in that way, they'll go through a wall for you. They'll also realize that you see them as unique individuals, which will help them to see the same in themselves.

If I don't have that kind of connection with a student, I'll try to find out if he or she has a family nickname. Or, I'll just ask them if they have a particular name they like to be called. That's a really important part of this process. My real name is James Russell, but I've never gone by Jim or James unless it was forced on me, as it was in Catholic school. Those teachers didn't seem to care about what was important to me. They simply followed some arcane set of rules, and I got my worst grades during those unhappy years.

The nickname has to be one that the child agrees on and is happy with. I used to call my nephew Charlie, "Cheese." One day he had the courage and good sense to say, "Uncle Rusty, I don't like that name. Could you call me 'Chunk' instead?" I was more than happy to oblige, and it created a stronger bond between the two of us.

To really know something is to name it. Think about the pet names you have for those closest to you. My dad always called my mom "Kitten," and she called him "Cal." My ex used to call me "Ruskers," and I call my brother and best friend Mike, "Max." It may seem like a little thing, but I think you'll find that seeing your students as individuals is the best way to build respect in the classroom and in their hearts.

Other ways in which I build self-respect are noticing things about my clients, giving them honest and non-judgmental feedback, and focusing on the action, not the person. You'll see that I said "notice" and not "compliment." The point here is to be aware of the person, but not to make judgments. When a kid comes in with a new haircut, I notice it and move on. They may be trying out a new style or they may have been forced into it, but either way, I see it and I see them, and that's what's important.

I'm asked to attend a lot of amateur sporting events, plays, and other performances as part of my life as an uncle and my job as a counselor. Inevitably, the person who I came to watch will ask me what I thought. I will often say, "It was interesting," or comment about something I noticed in the game or the presentation.

I might say, "I noticed your intensity on the boards and the way you moved the ball," or "I noticed your costume. Did you make it?" The child will usually then start to tell me what they liked and didn't like about the event and I get a chance to listen to their experience of it, which is what's important to me in the first place. However, when I'm coaching or working with a client, I do offer my opinion and advice, always striving to focus on the action instead of the person.

I try to incorporate tactics such as these in my work with children. These concepts have paid huge dividends both in my ability to create meaningful relationships with these kids, and in helping them begin to have more respect for themselves and for others. Respecting oneself is the cornerstone of social competency, and students will learn to respect themselves and others when the adults in their lives stop telling them they can be whatever they want to be, and begin to notice the kids for who and what they are. Adults and kids must be willing to work with that to the best of their respective abilities. This also facilitates the process of getting kids to be more responsible for their actions, which we'll turn to in the next chapter.

Teacher

If you were to ask any of my past students what my favorite word is, they could tell you without having to think. If you were to ask my colleagues what my favorite word is, they could tell you without having to think. If you were to ask my principal what my favorite word is, he could tell you without having to think. If you were to ask my two children what my favorite word is, they could tell you without having to think. If you were to ask my friends what my favorite word is, they could tell you without having to think. If you were to enter my classroom or my home, you, a perfect stranger, would know my favorite word without having to think. All would respond with the word, "BELIEVE."

One of my students last year must have been bored with one of my lessons because right in the middle of it her hand flew up. I called on her and instead of offering a point relevant to the discussion at hand, she informed me that I had 37 "Believe" signs in the classroom. While it was inappropriate timing, I had to stop and just go, "Wow."

I started collecting and displaying the word "Believe" five years ago. It all started while watching the movie *Miracle*, which is about the 1980 U.S. Olympic hockey team. The movie is about that team's coach, Herb Brooks, a man with a teaching style very similar to my own (as I have been told on many occasions). Coach Brooks creates a unit that eventually understands that a team becomes a family. During one of the games, the players come down a long hallway leading to the ice. While doing so, they are tapping letters and memorabilia hung on a huge bulletin board. If I had to guess, they were probably letters from family members and friends offering love and support for the players. I was floored at the effect that this tapping action was having on the players. They were getting pumped up to do their very best. They were reminded that they are not just individuals, but a vital part of a team. Their faces told the stories of their families back home, cheering them on and holding them to the highest standards. That was how part of my "Believe" vision began.

The other half of the vision came at the end of the movie. After they beat the nearly perfect Russian team and won the gold medal, Kurt Russell (playing Coach Brooks) says that his team, a bunch of individuals coming together as one, finally learned the lesson he tried to teach them all along, and that was to believe. My vision was sealed.

I started that school year with the "Believe" theme, and I have never stopped using it. I plastered the word "Believe" all around my classroom. Everywhere a student would look, I had a "Believe" sign. Students, fellow teachers, and even my family members started giving me all different types of "Believe" signs to add to my collection. I would find just the right place to display it, and the bigger the sign, the better!

I also added my version of the "Believe" vision from the movie. Running vertically up the side of my classroom door is the magic word. The B is high on top and the E ends up at a height level of a typical 10-year-old. As my students go out my classroom door into the real world, they are required to tap the letter of their choice. They can take the non-challenging E, or they can reach and jump real high for the B. At the beginning of the year the B is a challenge and many miss time after time. But, by the end of the year, they are smacking it with confidence. Now, it might have to do with them growing taller throughout the year, but I like to think and preach that it is because they are learning to believe that they can do it.

I also require each of my students to design and create a "Believe" sign of their own on an index card on the first day of school. I then tape this card to their desk below their name tag. Before starting an assignment or a test I tell them to give it a little tap to activate their believing powers. Sounds dorky, but it works!

Another way that I work the magic phrase into my classroom is to ask the students to put their name on their paper and write the word "Believe" next to it . . . but only if they truly mean it. Sadly, there have been times when a child has decided not to write the word next to his or her name. Once, a very, very intelligent little girl in my class did this. At recess, I pulled her aside and asked her why she chose not to write "Believe" next to her name. She said, very honestly and frankly, that she messed up. She said that she had forgotten to study for the test and that she knew she was not going to do her best. I responded to her by asking her if she believed that she did her very best knowing that she did not study. Did she use her testing strategies? Did she apply what she remembered learning in class? She seemed confused, so I put it a different way. I asked her if she had ever studied for her NWEA standardized test. She said no. I asked if she believed that she would do her best on that test, even though she didn't study for it. She said yes. "Well," I responded, "then you need to understand that all you do in class, from day one until today, builds and brings you to this place. Yes, you could have done better on the test had you studied, but you didn't. So, now you just have to believe that you will do what you know you can do and not look back. Even if you score an F, if you believe that you have done your very best, at this very moment, then you mean it." I finished up the conversation by asking her if she wanted her paper back so she could write the word "Believe" next to her name. She said yes. I asked her if she would write it knowing that she really meant it. She said she would. Amazing sparkles came out of that little girl's eyes that day, or maybe it was just the reflection of the ones coming out of mine. I like to think it was a little bit of both.

Having students take accountability for their own work by allowing them to believe that they can do it is magical. I can't begin to count the number of times in the past four years that I have watched children truly receive and understand the power of believing in themselves. Some experts might call this self-esteem. I say it is self-discovery. Over time, if a child sees the power as their own, they no longer look for incentives from outside people. They still love specific praise, but they also know that they deserve their reward because of giving the task at hand their very best effort each and every time.

I have yet to find a situation that I cannot fit in the concept of believing in oneself. Problems on the playground? Believe. Respect issues? Believe. Character issues? Believe. Problems with a bully? Believe. Problems at home? Believe. Problems with schoolwork? Believe. Nervous jitters before a standardized test? Believe. Nervous teachers before a standardized test? Believe. Amazing!

Just as it is amazing to see a child accept the possibilities of my favorite word, it is just as frustrating when I discover that a child has yet to connect. I have my students for 180 days, and then I have to let them go. There has yet to be a year that I have won over each and every student in this area. There are always one or two kids that do not leave with the "Believe" sparkle in their eyes. They believe off and on throughout the year, but it never really sticks in their heads. I have found that these students generally have very, very poor home lives. It is as if they want to believe with all that they are and all that they have, but then life throws them a curve that squashes out the flame that they have worked so hard to light day after day in class. This used to really bother me, and it still does to a point, but I have had to learn to let it go. I continue to keep them in my thoughts, and I continue to believe myself that they will one day see the power of my favorite word.

Once you get children to believe in themselves you need to take it to another level, a much more difficult level. Students next need to learn to share their gift by believing in others. This actually comes quite naturally. Students see how believing in themselves makes them feel like they can do absolutely anything, and they begin to develop this internal "Believe" radar. They begin to spot nonbelievers everywhere.

It might be their parents or siblings at first, or it might be one of their friends at school or in the neighborhood. They begin to use the phrase, "C'mon you can do it . . . just believe in yourself."

I got to witness this last year at our school's annual wiffle ball tournament. One of the requirements of the tournament is to cheer on and encourage the members of the opposite team. My class had this down to a science. When they saw a nervous batter, they began chanting "Believe, Believe, Believe." I almost couldn't pitch through the tears in my eyes. The clincher, for me, was in the All-Star game, where a selected group of high-character students played against the staff of our school. When it was my turn to bat, I heard the "Believe, Believe, Believe" chant. When looking around I discovered it wasn't just my current class saying it to me, but it was many of my past students saying it as well. I don't think they were saying it because I needed it, but I think it was really a sign of respect and gratitude. I was so proud of them, but even more I was proud of myself, because I had succeeded as a teacher. I had taught them a lesson that would stay in their hearts forever, and one that they could share with others.

I will leave you with this last story and bit of advice. One day, I went to observe my daughter Emma in preschool, which had a room with an observation window that allowed parents to see and hear their child without being seen in return. My daughter, who had no clue I was watching her, was alone in the room with a little boy. There was a hula-hoop there. Emma had recently mastered hula-hooping at home, so she easily picked up the hoop and had instant success. The little boy, on the other hand, had yet to master the art of moving his hips just right. So, my sweet baby girl stopped her hoop and looked him dead in the eyes while smiling. I thought, "Oh no, she is going to make fun of this little boy," but instead she put her hoop down and asked the little boy if he wanted her to teach him how to hula-hoop. He must have said yes because she continued by saying, "Well, the most important part of hula-hooping is to believe in yourself." I just about hit the floor. My four-year-old daughter had caught the "Believe" bug and was now sharing it with others. There have been many moments similar to this since then, but I will never forget the warm feeling that came over me when witnessing this for the first time. This leads me to my final advice on this subject of belief: Model it. Say it a million times out loud. Plaster the word everywhere you can. But, most of all BELIEVE it and SHARE it! It matters, and it makes a difference.

CHAPTER 8

Responsibility

Counselor

My first year as a school counselor was a bit rocky. I went in with all the enthusiasm of a recent graduate. My head was full of information and ideas, but not the experience needed to know the difference between theory and reality. I was convinced that I'd found my calling, and even though others had tried in the past, I was different. I was going to take responsibility for everything, and things were going to get better as a result.

I'd meet with more children in a week than anyone ever had. My kids would see the light, start to find more success in class, and get along better with others. In between, I'd run games during recess, take over the morning TV show, and still find time to teach social skills lessons in every classroom that would have me. Things went pretty well for about a month. Then, the counseling referrals got to the point that every minute of my day was full, from 8 a.m. until 3:30 p.m., with only 15 minutes for lunch, and the referrals just kept coming.

I began getting short with the teachers who asked me for help. I also found myself unwilling or unable to watch kids perform in-classroom activities that I wouldn't have missed for the world only a short time before. I started to hear from teachers that my kids were still having problems in class, and that they weren't following direction or getting their work in on time. I assumed this was because I wasn't pushing hard enough in our one-on-one sessions. So, instead of letting them play games or going outside to shoot hoops, I prepared curriculum for each session that dealt with a problem area. I made them go over the sheets with me and complete them before we spent any time talking or hanging out.

Almost immediately, my sessions with these kids became power struggles, which were about as much fun as trying to control a bucking horse by holding its tail. I couldn't understand what was happening. I had good intentions. I had tools that the students needed. I was anxious to impart this wisdom so they could learn and grow.

During my next advisory meeting, I told my supervisor and mentor what was going on. She talked to me about the process, and how I was a part of a much bigger picture. She helped me see that I needed to do what I was good at, and let other people provide the other pieces. In that way, together, we help move a child forward. This wasn't about me as much as it was about the process. If I could let go of my attachment to the results, it would make things a lot easier. In short, I needed to take responsibility for my own well being and for the things I could control, and leave the rest to the process.

Learning to take responsibility for oneself is not simply about admitting mistakes, although that is an important component, especially for young children. Responsibility is about setting boundaries and not trying to be all things to all people. Most important, it's about accepting and incorporating life circumstances that happen along the way.

One of the first clients I ever worked with was a young person who had been abused by a babysitter every day for more than a year. This person came to me, told me this story, looked at me, and said, "What are you going to do about that?" My response was immediate. I said, "It doesn't matter what I do with this information. What matters is what you're going to do with it, and how you're going to incorporate it into the rest of your life."

I couldn't change what happened, nor could I allow it to affect me to the point that I felt so sorry for this person that I bought into their victimhood.

Let's be honest, some of our kids have it rough, to say the least. I've worked with students who have been beaten and abused, raised in addictive households, and had struggling parents with very low social skills who had done little to prepare their child to succeed.

These students come from places that I'd be leery to drive through, and they have experienced things that I've only read about. One year, I worked at a middle school. Of the 24 students I met with, 10 had had at least one close relative murdered, and three had seen a person killed in their neighborhood. There is nothing we can do about that stuff, any more than we can change the families and the circumstances that formed us.

Good or bad, we all have issues with which we must deal. One of the most important ways we can teach children to become more responsible is to not allow their situation to affect us in a way that lowers the bar of expectation.

The trait that I appreciate most in my father is the high set of standards he set for his children. At the time, I didn't appreciate it. Quite frankly, I thought he was a pain. I came to realize that because he refused to settle for anything less than our best, we learned to push ourselves further and realize our potential.

As a coach, I know that if I set a high standard from the beginning, my players will reach for that standard, and if I don't, they won't. To do that, I have to be prepared and focused. I also have to be willing to admit when I'm wrong.

Last year, my nephew Charlie played on my seventh-grade AAU basketball team. We were competing in a tournament and had to win three games to get the championship trophy. We beat a good team to start the day, beat an average team in the afternoon, and only needed one more. The team we played last was not as good as the other two but that didn't deter me from coming out hard and trying to run them off the court. About 10 minutes into the game, I could see Charlie was struggling with something. So, I took him out and asked him what was up. He couldn't answer me, so I pressed on. We easily beat the team by 20 points to win the tournament.

Several days later, Charlie told me why he had been upset during the game. He thought I had been pushing too hard against an inferior team. In his opinion, we should have slowed it down, ran our offense, and treated our opponent with more respect. My first inclination was to blow him off, but I later realized I didn't feel good about that game.

The next day at practice I talked to the team about it, and told them that there are times when winning on the scoreboard and winning the game are two very different things. I apologized for not handling the situation differently. Most of the kids were looking at me like I was crazy, but leading by example is the key to teaching anything of value.

Early in my counseling career, I was finishing up some work in my office when I noticed some college students using the basketball courts at my elementary school. For security reasons, they weren't supposed to be there until after all the kids had gone home. I went out and told them in no uncertain terms that they had to leave. One of them mouthed off.

While a bunch of my kids stood around and watched, I went ballistic, yelling at the guy and threatening to call the police. They finally left, but I got called into the principal's office, a place where, ironically, I've spent a good deal of my time. The principal was very upset at what had happened. She wanted me to acknowledge that I'd overreacted, and sign a letter that would go into my personnel file. I told her she was wrong, and that I was just doing what needed to be done. We went back and forth for about 20 minutes until there was a knock at the door, and one the kids I worked with came in.

I'd met with this boy earlier that day because he'd been accused of hitting another boy, and we were trying to get him to tell the truth and apologize. Anyway, he walks in, looks the principal right in the eyes and says: "I did hit Jimmy, and I'll tell him I'm sorry when I see him tomorrow." The principal thanked him for his honesty, at which point he spun on his heels and skipped out of the office, apparently feeling much lighter than he had when he came in.

Before the door even closed, I admitted that I'd overreacted, and signed the letter. That little man taught me it's one thing to talk the talk, but it's a whole other thing to live up to our own expectations. When it comes to responsibility, or any of these skills, the kids are watching us much more than they're listening to the words that come out of our mouths.

What do we do if the kids in our care don't stand up and admit their mistakes? How do we teach them to be more responsible? One of the main complaints I hear from educators is that we can't hold kids accountable anymore. We spoke about that earlier in the book, but that was related to external punishment, and in that sense the educators are right. However, when we build relationships, holding students accountable is possible because they care about us and they know we care about them.

As Tammie mentioned in a previous chapter, we have all had a respected adult tell us that they are disappointed in us. This can have a much bigger effect than any punishment. If a child won't admit to something, then I tell the student what I think about it, and how it affects me. I can hold them accountable without them having to do a thing. If I have a relationship with them, then I focus on what I'm going to do as a result of their choices. I can only control my own behavior, so teaching responsibility must start and end with that. If I'm waiting for someone else to change for me to be happy, I'm not going be very happy.

Tammie is going to talk more about her system of rewards and punishments later in this chapter, and she will give you concrete examples of how this works. She will tell you that none of these ideas work unless you've built a relationship with the child first. She will also say that you teach responsibility by creating a structured environment that works for you and that makes the expectations clear. In short, you need to help your students establish and maintain effective boundaries.

Boundaries are powerful tools for teaching responsibility. We can't be all things to all people, and boundaries help establish the lines between where we end and other people begin. This may sound easy to do, but it's not.

Children who grow up in challenging situations often have very poor boundaries. At-risk families are characterized by chaos caused by uncertainty and by fuzzy lines of demarcation between the adults and children. It's called being enmeshed. The members of these families have no idea where one person ends and the other begins. So, at school, one of the best things we can do is to create environments that are structured to avoid confusion about roles and expectations.

Children need structure. Even though they might clamor for more freedom, they feel most secure when they know what's expected of them and what's going to happen next. It's not only children who benefit. I do better with structure in my life. I like to shoot from the hip when I'm speaking in public, because it makes it more real. In my day-to-day life, however, I rely heavily on routine. I'm a creature of habit, and good habits are one of the best ways to develop responsible behaviors. Boundaries create a sense of security by building on habit and routine, and by making it clear who's who and what's what.

Responsibility involves admitting mistakes, accepting and incorporating life circumstances, setting effective boundaries both personally and professionally, and not trying to be all things to all people. Teaching this skill involves admitting our own mistakes, not accepting excuses, and having high standards. By focusing on what we can control and by creating a predictable environment where it's safe to fail forward, we foster and teach responsibility. We also lay the groundwork for resiliency, which we'll turn to in the next chapter.

Teacher

One of my favorite character traits to teach is that of responsibility. This is a trait that many, including myself, can never seem to master. Therefore, it is a constant challenge, and I love a challenge. For kids, it is even more difficult. Kids thrive on rules and accountability. They hate it and love it at the same time. In today's world, kids need to be taught responsibility over and over again. They need to be held accountable for their actions, and they need to understand that all choices have consequences, good or bad.

My classroom expectations/rules are the six character traits, each of which I simply write with the word "be" in front of them:

- Be careful
- Be responsible
- Be respectful
- Be fair
- Be a positive and active citizen
- Be trustworthy

During the first few days of school, we take an in-depth look at how each of these traits actually applies to a classroom. I get on the computer, project a blank screen with the trait written in bold letters in the center, and I write as my students brainstorm about what that trait looks like, sounds like, acts like, etc. Finally, I print it and post it up in the room.

For example, let's look at the trait of responsibility. In the classroom, I want my students to understand that this means to do their homework, bring back parent papers, have all their school supplies ready to go, keep a clean and orderly desk, follow the class expectations, and so on. It is important to write these specifics on each poster, because later, if and when they make a negative choice, I like to have them go to the posters and read whatever trait they messed up on as a review and reflection tool. I also have them copy the posters into their morning journal, as I am writing them up, for future reference. When my students break an expectation, I generally don't address the specific offense. Instead, I will often say, "Johnny, this is a respect issue," or, "Sally, this is a responsibility issue." By looking at the poster or in their journal, they are able to determine what specific behavior they need to change, all on their own. I have found that this gives the students a sense of accountability. If I scold them for not having done their homework (the specific behavior), they have not learned how to identify and link their behavior choice to a character trait. It is important for kids to see, over and over again, that their behavior choices right now create their overall character in the future. That is a very out-of-the-box concept for a child's mind, but it is imperative that the vocabulary and modeling start from day one.

I mentioned above that all choices have consequences, good or bad. This is true in my classroom. I try very hard not to play favorites, and to make sure that I hold each and every student accountable for his or her actions. However, that being said, I also realize that each student is a unique individual. Some students break the rules every day, sometimes even multiple times a day. Then there are those that NEVER break the rules, unless they are having a really bad day. I have learned over my 10 years of teaching that kids deserve fair consequences, but they do not deserve equal ones. Therefore, I do not create or post a set of standard consequences in my room. My consequences vary from situation to situation and/or from child to child. Some students need very little consequence to understand that a change in their behavior is needed and expected. In these cases, a one-on-one conference in the hall or a gentle reminder of a trait will often suffice. Others need stricter and more consistent consequences that may last over a shorter or longer period of time, such as a loss of privileges or alternative seating in the room. In using a fair-but-not-equal strategy of this kind, students quickly learn that you see them as individuals, and that this is how the real world really works.

My classroom management system is a monetary one. I start each kid off on the first day of school with $300 fake dollars and a wallet. I printed the money off the internet, and the wallet is a simple manila bank envelope that I buy at Office Depot. Students can earn money and they can lose money at any given time.

Let's first discuss the ways in which students can earn money. In my class, each child is given a weekly helper job. I usually have around 24 students, so I have to get pretty creative when it comes to inventing different jobs for them to do. I start with the standard ones: classroom banker, telephone operator, technology assistant, teacher helper, pledge leader, classroom pet feeder, line leader, door holder, etc. Then I move onto the more creative ones: pink chair sitter, poem of the week reader, star of the week, etc. These tend to be the favorites of the class because they find themselves getting to sit in a comfortable chair for a week, bringing in their favorite poem to share, or talking about the special items they brought from home (for when they are star of the week). The most important job, however, is the reserve person. This person has to do any and all jobs that are assigned to someone who is absent on that particular day. The students get paid for all of their "work." I find these jobs to be helpful as well, because they eliminate fighting over who gets to sit in the big comfy chair, for example. This also gives me the perfect answer when a student wants to share an item or pet with the class. I simply say, "That would be a great thing to save for when you are star of the week."

The students get paid $50 a week, and payday is on Friday. In paying them, I simply run down the job list out loud, and they tell me if they did their job every day, some days, or not at all. We decide on a fair paycheck amount, and my banker then pays them their wages. It takes about five minutes to do this, and I assign them new jobs for the following week at the same time. I simply post all 24 jobs on a bulletin board and then move each child's name down one spot each week.

I am often asked what I do if one of my students lies. My answer: nothing. Before I even start calling for jobs I remind them that this is a time to shine in the character trait area of trustworthiness. I explain to them that I trust them to tell me the truth, and that I believe in them to do the right thing. I also remind them of the word karma. Do I have kids that flat out lie? Of course. Do they eventually get caught? Most of the time. Again, this is an opportunity for gentle reminders and lots of modeling.

Let me give you an example. A couple of years ago, I had a little boy who was assigned the door holder job. I found myself having to hold the door a lot that week. When he said that he did it every day and deserved his full salary, I simply reminded him of a couple of times that I found myself holding the door. I stated to him that the door holder job is a tough one. It is easy to forget, because we go in and out of doors sometimes five times a day. I then ask him to take a minute and to decide on a fair price for his paycheck. At the end of the payment session, I came back to him and he requested a much more reasonable paycheck amount. See, you can't let them get away with cheating the system, but calling them a liar doesn't work well, either. It is a teaching process, and it takes time. Some kids are honest from day one, and others take longer. You have to give them grace, and you have to model grace as well. Some teachers say that when I allow them to lie, I am setting a bad example for the other students that tell the truth. I disagree. I am modeling the act of grace and forgiveness. I am also giving them the long-term lesson of karma. Again, it's all about being fair, but not necessarily equal. There are also times when my reserve person will pipe up during paycheck Friday. Sometimes, a child will say that he or she did the job every day, but the reserve will remind me that they did that person's job that week due to an absence. Because I don't pay students for doing a job during an absence, I then ask the reserve to gently remind the student who forgot that that child should not get a full paycheck for that given week. It is a moral lesson, and one can see how it is strongly linked with character education.

My students are required to purchase a planner/agenda on the first day of school. This is filled out together as a class at the end of the day. Students then take it home, share the daily happenings with their parents, and obtain a parent signature at the bottom. The next day, they bring their planner to our Character Circle meeting. When our meeting is over, they bring it up to me for a signature check. If they have one, the banker pays them $20. If they don't, they pay me $20.

Students also have ample ways throughout the week to earn money. For example, I might give out $50 for each book a child orders off the monthly Scholastic book order forms. I might offer $100 for a sheet that needs to come back with a parent signature on it the next day. I might also offer $100 for attending a family function with their parents that is going on at our school, such as skate night, a PTA meeting, winter carnivals, book fairs, or family fun nights. I have also been known to just walk around the classroom with a stack of $20s in my hand and reward anyone that is on task or participating in a class discussion. The best part about this system is that it is not set in stone, and that you can link absolutely anything to it and get positive results quickly.

Now, let's switch gears and talk about how students can lose money. There are only three ways that kids can lose their money in my class.

The first one I mentioned above: If their planner is not signed, it is an automatic $20 fine. Second, if they fail to complete their homework, it is generally a $50 fine for each missing assignment. Lastly, if they break an expectation, it is generally a $50 fine each time. I say "generally" on the last two, because as I mentioned earlier, this system is not set in stone. If Billy repeatedly forgets his homework day after day, then his fine is likely to go up to $100 or more for each offense. If Betty continually talks out in class without raising her hand, then her fine is likely to go up to $100 each time. I am very careful to give the student full and fair warning that this is going to happen. I almost always say that the next time this happens, the fine will go up. I also only do this larger fine for a period of time, possibly a week or two at the most. Then I drop it back down to the general fine amount. The bottom line is that the students create their own consequences. They can make positive choices and earn money, or they can make negative choices and lose money.

So, what do they do with their earned money? Their first priority is to use it to buy into field trips. I place a standard fee of $1,000 for a field trip. This may sound like a lot, but by the time a field trip comes up the students generally have thousands and thousands of dollars in their wallets. The reason I make them buy into their trips is because if they can't make positive choices inside the four walls of my classroom, then there is no way that I am going to take them outside of those four walls. This works amazingly well when trying to explain to a parent why the child is being given an alternative placement on the day of the field trip. The only person that the parents have to blame for this is their very own child. When I send home a field trip permission slip, I add an extra line at the bottom that says, "Oops, I will not be able to buy into this field trip, Mom and Dad, because I have not made very good choices lately." If the student can't pay the $1,000 the day the slip goes home, then he or she has to mark this box, and still obtain a parent signature. If the student makes positive choices in class, then there is absolutely no reason why he or she should not be able to buy into the field trip. Generally, I take my class on three or four field trips a year.

I also require my students to pay a monthly rental fee for their desk and chair. It is generally $25 for each, so a total monthly fee of $50 is due on the first of every month. Students that can't cover their rent sit on the floor or stand until they can pay. Does this link to the responsibility trait or what?

I also present other activities that they can buy into. As an example, for $500 I might offer the use of an iPod for a day, or the right to bring a stuffed animal to school. I might also auction off some sodas or candy bars every once in awhile. Students can vote to have extra recess on a nice day—for a price. I also charge a buy-in fee for any film or movie we view in class, even if it is educational. Of course, popcorn and a drink is an extra charge as well.

The key to making this system work is to offer incentives and rewards that they can buy into early in the year. That way they see how the whole system works. I have found that kids become very upset when they have to give up their hard-earned cash. They learn very quickly that if they are not careful, they might miss out on the fun stuff. The bottom line here is that everything extra has a price, just like in the real world. If they want to do the extras, they have to pay for it. Otherwise, they have to sit on the sidelines and watch.

Whenever I present this system to other teachers I always get the question, "What do you do if a child becomes broke and no longer cares about the system?" This does happen, and the solution is quite simple. Catch them doing well as often as possible, and reward them heavily. Get them cash as soon as you can. Have them clean the desk tops, and pay them. Have them run errands, and pay them. Have them help others, and pay them. If they remember to write their name on their paper, pay them. Whatever it takes, just get them some money. Otherwise, they do shut down and they become frustrated with the system. However, do NOT just give money to kids that do not have enough to buy into an event, especially a field trip. I never, ever help a child earn fast cash just so he or she can participate in an extra event. If they haven't earned it, then they don't deserve it, and I would be doing them a HUGE disservice if I enabled them in this way. Kids have to learn that the responsibilities are theirs and theirs alone, and they have to be held accountable for their choices. I can tell you this, children that get left behind on a field trip generally get their acts together real quick to avoid this happening ever again. Those that don't figure it out get left behind over and over again. It is THEIR choice.

Another question I often get is, "How do you prevent stealing?" First let me say this: Karma stinks. This is one of the first lessons I teach my kids during Character Circle. I tell them that I trust them to make good choices when it comes to the temptations of stealing money from others or the bank. I tell them that they might never get caught stealing all year long, but that they have to live with the truth, and that eventually everything comes full circle (i.e., karma). I do tell them that if I ever catch them touching anyone else's money or wallet, they will have to give that person all of their money. This does help.

As far as lost money or lost wallets, I tell the students on day one that their money is their responsibility. If they lose it, then they start over with nothing . . . just like the real world. I NEVER replace lost money. The only time I might, and I say might, replace money is if a parent calls me and tells me that they threw it away on accident or washed it with the dirty clothes or something like that. Generally, even in those cases my response to the parent is, "Oh dang it. I am sorry that happened to Nelly. I would be happy to give her a new wallet and the start-up money of $300, but I can't replace the entire amount. Nelly knows that it is her responsibility to take care of her money and I told her that the safest place for her wallet is at school in her desk. I hope that she makes a better choice next time." Choices . . . Consequences. I am also teaching Nelly and her parents that I don't give into parental pressure.

I have made it a point to never link my money system to a student's grades. It is a behavior system, not an academic one. Therefore, I never pay students for getting an A or take money away for getting an F.

This system works for me. I have learned to let the small stuff go, and to trust my kids. I don't worry about kids stealing or cheating the system anymore. I just don't have the time or the energy to waste on these thoughts. If a case comes up, then I deal with it. Otherwise, I just have to trust that they are honest and decent kids.

The only downfall of this system is that my students handle their money non-stop. The minute they have free time, they count it, organize it, and separate it. There are times that I find myself saying, "Anyone counting money during instructional time will be making a huge donation to the bank." That means I will take all of their money if they don't put it away immediately. This is a great skill for kids to work on. It is a simple Character Circle meeting topic: dealing with when it is appropriate and inappropriate to count your money.

I have found that the kids also love this system. It makes sense to them. It is real to them. They are given the power to make their own choices. They are held accountable in a way that eliminates embarrassing scenes or the loss of recess time. They simply make a choice, are told to review an expectation poster/journal, pay a fine, and move on. I don't report daily infractions to parents. It is quick. It is over. It is forgiven. It is real life.

Amazingly enough, for the most part, parents seem to love this system as well. I have even had parents tell me that they use it at home. Be prepared for parents that do not like it, however. This system holds their sweet, innocent child accountable, and many parents get upset at me because of it. At first, I used to question the money system and my fair-not-equal practices. However, I have now committed to it. It is my job to teach the trait of responsibility. I have to look at the long-term goal for all of my students. I have to get them to understand that their present choices create their future beings. Sometimes, this has to start with teaching the parent this concept before the child will learn it. I can't think of one case, however, where I have not won over the parent before the end of the year. They eventually learn to love, or at least accept, this system.

Kids need boundaries. They need rules. They need to be held accountable. They want it, even though they hate it. It works for them, and it works for me. It may not work for you. It is not the system that matters, it is what you do with it. You may have your own choices . . . consequences system. All I ask is that you link your system to consequences, not punishment. A system linked to punishment is designed to temporarily control a child's behavior. A system linked to consequences is committed to teach and model the six traits of character building. It is one that allows reflection time and puts a name on the behavior, not a label on the student. It is also one that allows for grace and forgiveness. I have yet to find a system that establishes and reinforces the responsibility trait better than this one in my classroom. It truly is a win-win situation. You will know what type of system you have in place by thinking and reflecting on this last statement: When my students walk out my classroom door for the last time, I know they are walking out with good character skills that will help them become better citizens in their world. Will yours?

CHAPTER 9

Resiliency

Counselor

I constantly daydream (or "visualize" for those of you into the self-help movement) of being interviewed on a national TV show after this book is published and more people begin to take note of the work we're doing. I'm sitting on the couch, trying to be calm, cool, and collected, when the host asks me how I'm dealing with all this overnight success. I see myself laughing and saying "Yeah, it's amazing. It only took 48 years to get here!"

What is success, and when do you know you've succeeded? I once heard that you can never really judge a person until after they're dead because you never know what they might do in those last moments. O.J. Simpson was "successful" for most of his life and is now considered a pariah. Bernie Madoff made a lot of money but now sits in jail despised by those who trusted him for a very long time.

When I think of success, I think of ordinary people I've met along the way who somehow find the strength to pick themselves up, dust themselves off, and keep going even when everything seems to be against them. Those are the ones who've bounced back from the inevitable bumps in the road that we all must learn to navigate, or which will eventually knock us off the path.

I also realize that living a life of value and purpose requires time. Overnight success is fleeting, but hard-earned passion is something that will not go away quietly. One of the last surprises my mom gave me before she died was a CD book set called, "I Hope You Dance" by Lee Ann Womack. The song on that CD focuses on appreciating the little things and learning to enjoy the journey. Mom always worried about me because it must have seemed like it was taking me a really long time to find my stride.

What that song says to me and what I've now come to understand is that everything I've been through had to happen to get me to where I am today. That's one of the greatest gifts my mother ever gave me—the ability to pick myself up and keep going. My mom, along with all the other important people in my life, taught me how to be resilient and to never quit on myself or my dreams.

The flipside was that as I focused more on myself, I began to isolate from other people. I began treating other people in my life as things instead of people. I had a tendency to see people in terms of what they could do for me rather than who they were. I didn't make an effort to enter into their world or be very empathetic to what they were dealing with. This isn't because I'm a bad person; it was just easier for me to do it that way. It was a defense mechanism that I developed over the years to keep myself "safe."

Growing up as a military brat, I lost friends on a regular basis. At some point I decided that it was just too painful to really get to know people only to lose them when the next moving date arrived. As I began to work with kids, however, I was able to open up again and that has led me to more satisfying and fulfilling relationships with peers as well.

Resiliency is the ability to come back from challenges, whether forced on you or self created. As I was doing research for this chapter, I came across Edith Grotberg, who identified five building blocks of resilience: trust, autonomy, initiative, industry, and identity.[6] So how can we bring these building blocks into the classroom and help those in our charge begin to build a foundation that will last a lifetime?

I've talked about trust, and how it is the basis of all relationships. Children who grow up in dysfunctional households have a very difficult time trusting others, especially adults, because they've been let down, neglected, and left to fend for themselves at a time when their brains are in the process of discerning what's safe and what's not.

The brain is an amazing machine but it works on a pretty simple premise, which is to categorize experience and then judge future similar experiences based on that earlier information. If a child grows up in a place where adults can't be trusted, that child's brain makes a note of it, and that becomes the lens through which other adult are viewed.

It's like when a child is bitten by a dog and develops a phobia of dogs going forward. The category, dog, is classified as dangerous and not to be trusted, even if it's obvious to everyone else in the room that the animal is docile. Please understand that this is a gross oversimplification of how the brain works and I'm not an authority on the subject by any means, but I think it serves our purposes here.

So how can we help? We help by being the one trusted adult on whom that child can rely. Resiliency research indicates that the presence of at least one caring adult is the most important factor in a child's ability to overcome even the most emotionally austere of early childhood experiences. In most cases, being able to rely on at least one adult allows the child to overcome years of fear and distrust.

For me, the key to becoming a trustworthy person in a child's life is to really listen. There is something very powerful in listening and being listened to. In every assembly, I ask the kids how many eyes they have and they yell, "TWO!" I ask how many ears they have and they again yell, "TWO!" Finally, I ask them how many mouths they have, and they yell, "ONE!" I tell them that if they learn to look and listen twice as much as they talk, the world will open up and share all of its secrets.

I realized the importance of listening and really paying attention in my first few months at Rosedale School. I began to understand that what these little souls needed was for me to just sit there for a few minutes once a week, make them the center of my attention, and really listen to what they were saying. When I did that, I heard things that were important to them, and I would make mental notes to follow up.

When a child told me of a trip to the fair or the lake in the coming weekend, I would ask him or her about it the next time we met. I've heard Tammie talk about how much she relies on her morning circle time to find out what's going on with her class, and she immediately makes notes so she can follow up. It's the small things, done in a minute, that often last a lifetime.

Creating a space where each child has a chance to talk about what's going on in his or her life, at least once a week, has worked well for me, even when I was only working with a classroom once a week over the school year. At the beginning of each class I taught, I'd take a few minutes to ask the kids to raise a hand if they had anything they wanted to share with me and the class. Almost every hand would go up. I would get a ton of useful information to help steer my conversations with them in the weeks to come.

Some teachers meet each child at the door with a handshake and ask them what's going on, while others use the morning circle and personally directed writing prompts to stay involved. It doesn't take much time to begin really connecting with your students on a personal level, and it goes a long way in establishing you as a trusted adult in their lives. Once children begin to trust more, they can take the next step and begin to exert some control over their lives and actions.

Autonomy is a feeling of independence and the ability to make decisions. William Glasser's Choice Theory[7] is based on the idea that motivation is internal. Glasser believes that all of us have basic needs we're trying to satisfy and which drive motivation, one of which is the need for autonomy.

Obviously, it would be impossible to allow children complete freedom to make choices about how they spent their time. Without the insight of long-range thinking (which doesn't emerge in children's brains until much later) most students will continually choose instant gratification over the delayed benefits obtained through necessary learning activities.

However, there are ways to give children freedom of choice while still meeting the requirements of the learning environment. The easiest way to do this is to have a number of alternative learning materials, all of which serve the same purpose. Then, have the class vote on which one they'd like to do. Have them pick which book to read at story time or which experiment to do for science. You can give them homework pages with a number of questions on them, and then let them pick which 10 they want to do.

If you're reading a chapter in class, the goal is to get the students to understand the material. There are several ways in which they can demonstrate this understanding. You can offer them the choice of writing a paragraph, making a slide show, or doing an oral presentation. The key is to give the students options about how to meet the requirements of the lesson, while still maintaining control over the content.

My favorite example of how this works was presented at a parent training I attended. Several of the parents expressed concern about how to deal with a child who was either reluctant to get dressed in the morning, or who would pick out inappropriate outfits. The facilitator explained that a good way to deal with this problem was to pick out two or three options, and then allow the child to select which combination to wear. He went on to caution the audience against worrying too much about whether the outfit the child selected matched. He said, "The key is that they're dressed appropriately for the weather and for the environment. What's more important at this point, having child who is dressed and ready to go, or having a child be the best-dressed kid in class?"

This also works well with consequences. When a child breaks a rule, you can offer that child a choice in how to make amends. If the child is disturbing the class, you can present a choice: Either follow along with the rest of the class, take a time-out, or sacrifice 10 minutes of recess time to do the work that's being avoided at that time.

We all have a job to do, but as with most things, there is usually more than one way to accomplish the task. Taking a few extra minutes to create choice in the classroom is one of the most powerful ways to teach children how to be autonomous, and to help them begin to exert some control over themselves and their environment. When this happens, children begin to see a connection between choices and outcomes, and how what they do affects who they become.

Initiative is the ability to take action. The inability to take action, which I refer to as learned helplessness, is a problem I see in many of the children with whom I work. I ask the parents of my basketball team to have their children speak to me directly if they have any questions regarding what they need to do to get better and contribute more to the team. The idea is not to cut the parents off, but to teach the players how (and with whom) to communicate when they have a problem or a question.

Too often, caring adults believe that the best way to help children is to solve their problems for them, but what this does is create the sense that problem solving is something "other" focused. It creates an external locust of control. This approach teaches children that they need other people to do something for them to overcome a challenge or feel better.

I saw this all the time when I was teaching domestic violence classes to adults. Most of the attendees held the belief that for them to make progress, their partner had to change. I don't know about you but I've wasted a lot of time waiting for other people to change. What I've learned is that it rarely happens. If I want something to be different, the only person I can control is me. I ask myself, "What do I need to do to change this situation or make it work?"

Obviously, when it comes to serious issues like children's safety, they need us to take action on their behalf. This also teaches the child that asking a trusted adult for help is a form of taking action, so there is benefit to adult intervention. However, asking a child what he or she can do to solve a problem, before getting involved, is critical to helping the child understand that things change and get better when they take action, not when they wait for others to do it for them. It also helps the child to see that hard work pays off.

Industry is learning how to work for something. Like initiative, it can be severely undermined by adults who are trying to help. As I said before, the self-esteem movement believed that the way to get the most out of a child was to lavish him or her with praise, and to treat everyone the same. Two questions come to mind, however: First, if we don't teach children how to work for something, who will? Second, who's going to be there to give them unearned praise and reward once they become adults?

A big part of this process is to redefine hard work. I hear adults constantly telling children they have to work really hard in life. What's hard? They need to do their homework and their chores, but we're not talking about breaking rocks here. I tell kids that work is simply time plus effort. Whatever we spend our time and efforts on grows in our lives, and what we don't spend time and effort on shrinks.

"Hard" is a relative term and probably prevents kids from trying new behaviors that will eventually, over time, add up to good habits that they can rely on to get things done. It reminds me of New Year's resolutions and why so many people fail to keep them for even a month. The script usually goes something like this: I make a resolution to lose 20 pounds, so I join a gym. On the first day I go for two hours, work out on every machine, and come home thrilled by my efforts. The next day, I'm so sore that I can't even get off the couch, so I miss a few days. I return by the end of the week, but this time I pull something and am in pain for the next two weeks. By the time I recover I've given up on the whole thing and find myself back to business as usual. I think most gyms stay open because of people who buy memberships in January that go unused.

It takes awhile to put on 20 pounds, and it takes time to get it off. Time plus effort equals work (and not necessarily hard work), and this is what we need to do to make things happen. The best way to teach industry is to equate time and effort with outcomes. If we can equate classroom rewards and privileges to effort, we'll teach children how to work for something, and then they will begin to see the kinds of work that they like to do, which leads to a better sense of who they are. In turn, they begin to establish their own identity.

Identity is a sense of who we are and where we're going. For most of us, this is a life-long process, but it can be facilitated in the early years by helping children identify the things that they are good at and then building on those strengths. As with all the aforementioned skills, honesty and awareness are the keys. The more aware we are of children in a variety of situations, and the more honest we are with them about what we see, the better able they are to start to develop a sense of self.

Resiliency is the ability to fall, get back up, and try again. Trust, autonomy, initiative, industry, and identity are the tools that help a child learn how to be resilient in the face of life challenges. Whatever you can do to help facilitate these skills along the path for a young person, the better prepared they will be for the road ahead. That's why SchoolToolsTV was born. In the next chapter, we'll finish up by talking about the show and how it became the vehicle for me to bring "The Other 3 Rs" back into the classroom.

Teacher

When I think back on the mentors in my life, I remember my sixth-grade teacher, Mrs. Laird, in particular. I am friends with her to this day, and there is one thing I particularly remember about her. She was the one teacher who took me aside and in no uncertain words told me to sit down, shut up, and stop making excuses for my future. It must have hit home because I sat down, shut up, and became the teacher that I knew I always wanted to be. We all have these kinds of stories. There is always one person in our life, usually an adult, who has helped us grow up and become positive professionals.

When I think about the choice I have made to become a character-driven teacher, I think about the lives that I touch. I want to be that adult for the kids in my class. I have been teaching long enough now that students are beginning to come back and visit me. It is a true honor for me to still be in their lives, and to listen to them tell stories about what they remember learning or doing while in my classroom. This is why I take the time. This is why I go the extra mile. This is why I stick out my professional tongue to the critics that say my job it to just teach my students academics. This is why I am a teacher.

There are many opportunities during a regular school day to take a valid interest in what my students are thinking and learning. When we are in reading groups and discussing a chapter that we've read, I always ask character-trait-type questions. One of the best ways to do this is ask the question, "If you were a teacher filling out a report card on the character _____, what grade would you give him or her in trustworthiness (or whatever trait you might pick)?" It is amazing what kids see in this area. It is often not what I see at all. They often end up in a debate with other group members, and the empathy piece comes out full force. If you, as the teacher, just sit back and listen, and I mean really listen, you will discover entire underlying messages about each child in your classroom.

Kids wear their feelings on their sleeves, and they often admit their own shortcomings or thoughts about issues happening at home when given the chance to talk about someone other than themselves. For example, when we were reading the book *Rescue Josh McGuire*, which is about a little boy whose father is an abusive drunk, I must have discovered at least six children that were living in similar situations just by listening to the empathy piece they had for Josh or the father. It gave me insight into their otherwise very protected worlds. You could just tell that they were talking from their hearts. It is important to discuss the academic/ comprehension questions in reading group, but I find a much greater learning process going on when I add in the character-trait component. I know who has read and understood the chapter by the evidence they bring up to defend their opinions in the debate and discussion.

Another way I handle daily character education is during my Character Circle time. There are a million picture books that have character issues in them. We all know about the Berenstain Bears and Clifford, but those are not going to work with my fourth graders. So, I have to dig a bit deeper. I have a character library now of about 30 to 40 really good books suitable for fourth graders; you can find a list of some of my favorites in the Appendix at the back of this book. Recently, I discovered a huge secret. If you want really good character books, look for ones written about Native Americans. These books have amazing character traits built into them, especially ones that tell a story passed from generation to generation. Wow! I have also found that it is pretty easy to find some great literature about bullying.

The bottom line is that there are books about almost any possible situation that you are dealing with in your classroom, or that a child is dealing with at home. Last year, many of my students lost close relatives during the school year. They kept sharing their thoughts about these sad events during feelings time, and it was really bothering them. I decided to act upon it. I found a book about losing family members and the grieving process, and read it at Character Circle time. I then created a bulletin board that said "Celebrate Life!" For the next week, I invited the kids to bring in mementos or pictures of loved ones who had passed on. The students would then share their items with the group, and then I would hang them up on the board. We had photos, jewelry, trinkets, and more surrounding us for the entire week. I also had Rusty video-conference into my class to talk about his mom's passing and how he celebrates her life. We talked about how it is important to respect those that have passed away by celebrating their life instead of focusing on the fact that they are no longer with us. This activity created a strong bond between those that shared and those that listened to their stories, including me. It was a very touching week.

At any rate, I read these stories at our Character Circle meetings, and then I have the kids do three or four activities revolving around the book and its messages. I might spread this out over the entire week or just do it all in one day. I also make sure to place all the character books I read on a special display shelf. I have noticed that kids love to go back and re-read these types of stories during their independent reading time. I keep them out year round.

The easiest way to fit character education into my day, however, is to watch Rusty at SchoolToolsTV. Rusty will explain the show in detail in the next chapter, but let me say that I love it! There is always a character issue to talk about, a weekly manner to discuss, and a weekly Bully Byte. One activity I do with my kids is to have one volunteer draw a visual of the Bully Byte each week. I then string them up in a line on my wall following a sign that simply reads, "Bully Bytes." When kids come to me with bully issues in class, on the playground, or at home, I simply ask them what Bully Byte they decided to use and how it worked for them. They tend to shift their vision to this wall and take a look at their choices. Saying this over and over again, and having a visual reminder of what Rusty tells them, makes my job a lot easier. My kids don't get to just tattle to me. They have to come to me with a strategy they used to try to stop the behavior on their own first. If they don't come with one, I remind them that I am only here to help them after they have tried using a Bully Byte and it has not been successful. Of course this does not count if someone is being seriously hurt or threatened, and they know that. This is for all of those situations in which kids just run to us to solve their problems for them. I always tell them that one day I will not be there for them, and their parents will not be there to solve their problems. They have to learn strategies on how to deal with bullies around them all on their own.

It is also quite easy to tie in character education on or around holidays. I have done entire character-based days around Martin Luther King, Jr.'s birthday, Halloween, Labor Day, Red Ribbon Week, and so on. It is pretty powerful when you divide up your class on MLK, Jr. Day into "blacks" and "whites." It is even more amazing when you transform your entire day to resemble that time period, like posting signs that say, "Whites only," or give out special privileges or snacks to only the kids labeled "white." I've had kids in tears because they felt so bad for the kids labeled "black." Mid-day I had them switch roles. It about killed me to treat the "black" kids with so little respect and downright rudeness. The discussion at the end of the day, however, was all worth it. Kids poured their guts out. They had a whole new attitude about history and how this world has emerged. The most interesting discussion, however, was about me. They were not shy in telling me how mean I was, and how unfairly I had treated them. I had a hard time reassuring them that it was all an act, and that I had to be that way to make the activity seem real. I finally was able to, but they were pretty shell-shocked to see their character-driven teacher go against everything she preached.

Red Ribbon Week is one of my favorite times to focus on character education. It is easy to link issues involving drug and alcohol abuse with the traits of trustworthiness, caring, responsibility, respect for your body and others, and being a positive citizen. You can get some pretty amazing guest speakers during this time as well. I have had undercover DEA officers, drug teams and dogs, teenagers that are dealing with drug issues, former gang members, parents of kids that have been caught drinking, and probation officers come in and talk to my students. Of course, they talk about their jobs and their life stories, but the one requirement I make with these speakers is that they have to address issues of character, whether it is the son who has lost his mother's trust or the DEA officer who had to pass extensive character background checks to maintain his or her employment.

All week, we talk about the character of people that use and abuse drugs. I talk about how their poor character choices generally start at my students' ages, 9 or 10. I talk about how their choices in this matter affect not only their lives and their character, but also their families and friends. We take the time to watch the episode of *Little House on the Prairie* where the Albert character gets hooked on drugs and ends up stealing from the town doctor; running away from his father, friends, and home; and even slapping his teacher in class. This episode really does a great job of showing withdrawal symptoms such as tremors and hallucinations. I don't hold a lot back with my fourth graders, because they need to know what the world without positive character choices looks like.

For the past two years, I have ended Red Ribbon Week with a field trip to the local jail. We get the whole tour. My students walk by the cells. They see the inmates, male and female. They see and smell the crappy food. They see the stacks of underwear that all the inmates have to share. They get yelled at by the inmates, usually including profanity. They see the maximum-security facility where the pedophiles live, and I tell them that these are people that might be in their Internet chat rooms, pretending to be their age. They see the weapons that the officers use to keep the inmates in line. They get to sit in the time-out chair with restraints on their arms, legs, and waist, along with a spit mask over their heads. They get handcuffed. They see the booking room and the drunk tank. They get to experience the god-awful smell of puke and poop that lurks in the building. They see the courtroom, where they video-conference from the jail with the judge. They see it all. It becomes very real to them, and they don't ever want to go back. They aren't too young to see this. They aren't too young to be scared. They aren't too young to understand that I take them there because I care about them and their futures. I realize, and make them realize, that it all starts right now. The officer leading the tour tells them that almost 90 percent of the inmates began making negative choices when they were 9 or 10. That hits home!

I bring in guest speakers who have abused drugs or alcohol because I also want the kids to see that even if they do mess up and make poor choices, they can still bounce back and have a successful life. I want them to hear stories about kids their age getting sucked in by peer pressure and succumbing to the world of drugs. I want them to see kids who have been in juvenile hall and came out better people. Most important, I want them to understand that these are not bad people, but that they just made really bad choices. They got help, and are now productive members of society. This is an amazing time to talk about successful athletes that have substance abuse problems. There are many videos and articles on the Internet that tell such stories. Good people . . . bad choices.

The story of how Red Ribbon Week even got started is pretty amazing in itself. I tell this story on the first day of the week. I print a picture of Enrique "Kiki" Camarena[8] and hang it up on my front board. We talk about how wearing our red ribbons honors this man, who died in the fight against drugs so kids like them can be safe in their neighborhoods. It is a powerful story.

It has been said that kids today begin making poor choices at earlier and earlier ages. They have no clue as to how those choices will affect the rest of their lives. In the past, our parents tried to warn us about these dangers, and we thought they didn't know what they were talking about. It's the same with kids today. However, if kids can find just one adult to lead them, educate them in a way that they understand and can buy into, and never leave their side when it comes to accountability, then we can save that child from destroying his or her future at a young age. I want to be that adult for my students. That is what drives me to teach the way I do. I don't believe my job is to teach my students everything in their textbooks. I believe my job is to prepare them for their lives ahead—today, tomorrow, a year from now, or whenever. It is my job, as a teacher, to guide them away from danger and to teach them how to keep themselves safe. I take my job very seriously. The question is, do you? After all, a child's life is at stake.

CHAPTER 10

SchoolToolsTV

Counselor

September 11, 2001 is a date that few will ever forget. Those of us who are old enough will always remember where we were when we saw the towers come down and began to understand what had happened. It came to my consciousness when I pulled up to the Skyway House in Chico that morning. The Skyway House was a residential treatment facility for men dealing with addiction issues, and I was a counselor there.

Normally when I arrived, the guys would be taking their morning walk down the long driveway that connected the house with the main road. But on that day, no one was out walking. When I reached the front of the Spanish-style building that 10 to 15 residents called home for six months, I could see why. They were all gathered around the big, recently donated, console TV in the garage. When I got out of my car, they told me what was happening.

The first thing that came to my mind, after the initial shock and disbelief, was a concern about whether or not I'd be having class that night, or if I even wanted to go. You see, 9/11 was more than just a day I'll never forget because of what ended, it's also a day I'll never forget because of what began. My first counseling class was scheduled to take place that night.

Class went on as planned, and obviously, the majority of that evening was spent talking about what had happened. It was a chance for all of us to grieve and to think about what we were preparing to do in the light of a changing global reality. What really stuck with me were the words of our instructor, who told us that we would have to become innovators if we were going to change the culture brought about by standardized testing. It was up to us to bring school counseling back from the edge of obscurity.

He told us that schools were becoming increasingly focused on outcomes and results that were driven by data. He cautioned that counseling was considered a "soft science," and that practitioners were having a hard time coming up with empirical proof of why it was valuable under NCLB. Finally, he said, "The days of being able to keep a job because the kids like you and the teachers think you're a nice person are gone. The teachers have less time to spare for things like counseling and social skills, and you're going to have to figure out new ways to get the message out."

I was told that I had to be an innovator and a "change agent," which was the cool catchphrase to use at the time. I bought in hook, line, and sinker, and it's not hard to understand why. I was very comfortable in the role of the outsider who questions the status quo and authority in general. You see, one of the reasons I'm good at what I do is because I'm not unlike the kids I'm attempting to reach.

Being a military brat and a Catholic has taught me a good deal about the difference between accepted wisdom and the real thing. I've met enlisted people and general officers, and I learned quickly that rank doesn't mean a thing when it comes to being a good leader of troops or getting a job done. It was even more obvious when it came to my religious tradition. Let me preface this by saying that I'm still Catholic to this day, although I don't participate in the organizational part of the faith. Nevertheless, I'm very proud of my religious background and what it's meant to my development.

The experience that allowed me to clearly see the difference between organized belief and truth happened in 1974 at St. Bernadette's School in Silver Springs, Maryland. As at all good Catholic schools, we student went to church a lot. I always wondered if it was to remind us of what was important or to put a little scare into us. Hell is a great motivator for keeping young boys and girls in line.

A new boy had joined our class that week from India. I don't remember his name but I do know that he wasn't Catholic. His parents must have thought that a Catholic school was a better option than the public system, so he joined our class in the middle of the year. I happened to sit next to him in church one day. Once I realized that he didn't know what was going on, I took it upon myself to share all the wonders of my faith with him. I told him when to stand and when to kneel, and I even took him to Communion and told him what to do when he got up there.

After mass was over, I was heading back to class when one of the nuns grabbed me by an ear and started to fill it with a tirade about how much trouble I was in for talking during church. I couldn't wait until she was finished so I could tell her the good news. I said, "But Sister, he's not Catholic so I was just telling him what to do so he'd realize how cool being Catholic really is." She smiled briefly and then got this look on her face like I'd just shot the pope. She proceeded to yell at me, "And you allowed him to receive the Eucharist without having gone through First Communion?" Needless to say, the rest of that afternoon was spent cleaning desks as the nuns stood around and gossiped about what I'd done.

The whole time I was scrubbing away, I couldn't help but think that the God of my understanding would have wanted that young man to join us in the celebration. What the nuns didn't understand was the difference between procedure and common sense. It reminds me a lot of what's been going on in education ever since NCLB became law. Something needed to be done about our public education system, but we've thrown the baby out with the bath water and decided that education is about high-stakes testing and preparing individuals to work in a consumer-driven economy instead of developing real intelligence that can discern the difference between common sense and common practice.

I wanted to do something to help swing the pendulum in the other direction and get it closer to the middle path. SchoolToolsTV started out as my thesis project and eventually became that something. Through this program, I was able to grab the attention of the entire school for several minutes each day. It was a way for me to be an agent of change, if you will, and publicize our schoolwide expectations for behavior while giving students little tips about how to work more effectively in class and get along with others in the playground.

As with most things, the idea wasn't really new. I was raised on Saturday morning cartoons, back when we only had the three major networks from which to choose, and what I remember most was *Schoolhouse Rock!* I can't tell you much about Bugs Bunny or the Road Runner, but I do remember "Conjunction junction, what's your function" and "I'm just a bill, and I'm sitting here on Capitol Hill." For some reason, these ideas stuck with me. I wanted to offer kids the same kind of common-sense ideas that I'd grown up with, but were sorely lacking in many of the young people I was working with.

I broke the program down into five main skills, one for each day of the week, and then into three sub-groups for the first three weeks of each month. The last week focused on an important issue like bullying or cooperation. It started with Motivation Monday, which was about motivation at school and at home, including homework and chores. Teamwork Tuesday dealt with being a team player, getting along with others, and asking for help. Wellness Wednesday talked about diet, exercise, and relaxation techniques. Thoughtful Thursday focused on self-esteem, positive thinking, and responsibly. Friendship Friday dealt with how to make, keep, and be a good friend. That part of the show has morphed into Find Out Friday, and now we have a quiz that reviews what we've talked about and gives the kids a chance to show what they've learned.

The show was a hit from the very beginning, but what amazed me the most was how quickly the students learned the closing poem I'd created, almost as an afterthought. Within a few weeks, you could hear almost every kid in the school following along with me as I closed each show with the mantra: "Feelings are a big deal but they come and they go. Bullies are real but we can say no. It's up to us to make a choice. It's up to you to find your voice. Peace out little diamonds, the rest is still unwritten. I hope you have a fantastic day." Not only did they know it by heart, but they wanted to recite it with me every time I went into their classroom or when they wanted to make contact with me in the yard. I was connecting with the entire school population and teaching them social skills through a medium that they loved, and it was all happening in only one minute a day.

The other really amazing thing that happened was that teachers started to tell me that the one minute was turning into five or 10 minutes of classroom discussion about the topic of the day. Many were also using it as their writing prompt. They shared with me how it helped them focus on their needs in the classroom, and how it also made it easier for them to talk about these important topics with their classes.

There's a huge amount of positive wisdom in the minds and hearts of our teachers, but they'd been told to stick to the curriculum and teach to the test for so long that they'd stopped focusing on other things. What was happening was that the "Morning Minute," as it was first called, created a place to talk about manners, social skills, and pro-social behavior in a preventative way, and it provided tacit permission to do so. It was working and the kids and the teachers loved it.

Not only did I have my thesis project, I also had an idea that I could turn into something that could reach more people and make an even bigger impact. Rancho Respecto was born the summer following my graduation in 2003. I'd been working in the career center at the local community college for one of my favorite bosses of all time, Merlyn Newlin. It's interesting to me how all my mentors up until Mrs. Thelkeld had been men, and ever since then have been amazing women.

Merlyn liked was I was doing and introduced me to the person in charge of the video production facilities at the college. He agreed to give me five days of studio time to shoot 100 episodes of my show, and then give them to me on a DVD that I could hand out to other schools. I had always had kids on Rosedale TV who helped me out and talked about what I was saying, so I figured I'd need that with the new version as well. A couple of friends of mine had kids who were the right age, one boy and one girl, and they were thrilled with the idea of being on "TV." We made a set out of stuff I'd bought from a local thrift store and several bails of hay. We filmed for six or seven hours a day for an entire week. My little co-stars did pretty well but it was not easy for them.

We ended up getting it done and the DVD looked pretty good. The only problem was that teachers told me it took too much time to set up the TV and put in the DVD. Each episode was actually about 90 seconds long at that point, so it wasn't exactly a "Morning Minute." In response to these comments, I realized that if this was going to work, it needed to be shorter and easier to use. Hello, Internet.

As with most things in life, timing is everything. At that time, schools were getting grant money to put in new computers networks, and more computers were popping up and being used in the classrooms in my area. I'd left Rosedale by then and moved onto a job with the Glenn County Office of Education. It was there that I met my next professional mentor, Merrilee Johnson. My mom was going through the final stages of her terminal illness at that time, and Merrilee was there for me every step of the way. When I first found out that my mom was dying, I thought seriously about leaving California and moving back east to be closer to her. Mom told me not to do that, however. She knew that she didn't have a lot of time left and that I was just starting to get some traction in my new career. Merrilee helped me through these decisions as well, and gave me a leave of absence so I could take care of my family issues. When it was all over and I returned, Merrilee welcomed me back with a full-time position for the upcoming school year.

I'd been working three jobs for the previous few years just to make ends meet, and this opportunity finally provided some job security and the health insurance that my mom was always so worried about. The position was as a social skills educator providing Second Step lessons in classrooms around Butte County. Merrilee encouraged me to talk to the technology people in the county about my show, which I was now filming by myself on a weekly basis. It was being broadcasted on my first website, www.MorningMinute.tv.

At first the site was blocked at a majority of schools, but the I.T. folks soon provided access to more teachers. As a result, I now had 30-40 classrooms in different schools over three different counties all watching the show. This grew to as many as 50 schools by the time SchoolToolsTV began.

Today, the show is watched by thousands of children in hundreds of classrooms all across the United States. We even have a few schools in Canada, Australia, and a Department of Defense-run school in Italy. How did it happen? I can offer two primary reasons.

First, I did what I'd been taught to do and what I've been talking about throughout this book: I believed in myself and had enough self-respect to find my unique voice. I'd taken responsibility for myself and for making the changes I needed to make to create a life that made sense to me. I was resilient enough to bounce back from some really difficult things like my divorce, my mom's death, and all my failed attempts to get my life and SchoolToolsTV off the ground. I never quit on myself or gave up on my beliefs. Finally, I had trusted adults along the way who helped me and reminded me of what's important, primarily the need to always be true to myself.

Second, it happened because of caring teachers who were tired of working in a high-stakes, high-stress test environment with kids who had trouble learning even if they wanted to because they didn't have the basic skills necessary for success. These teachers, like my co-author Tammie Erickson, embraced the program and shared it with others.

I'm certainly not done growing and changing, and neither is the resource that SchoolToolsTV plans to become. We envision a "counselor in the classroom" type resource that will help teachers and students deal with social skills deficits in the same way that we help them with reading or math. But the most important thing we do, and the reason why this site is going to continue to be a part of the educational horizon for years to come, is that we help teachers create even more powerful and positive learning relationships with their students. We make it easier for everyone involved to get their work done and grow as human beings.

This book is a big part of these next steps, and I can't thank you enough for taking the time to read it. My hope is that you use some of the ideas expressed here in your own life and with the children you already do so much for each and every day. You are the true heroes, the boot on the ground, that make it all work. I couldn't be prouder to say that we work together in some small way, and it only takes a minute a day. Peace out diamonds, the rest is still unwritten.

Teacher

I have mentioned before that allowing students to see that you are a real person is a sure way to create a genuine relationship with them. One of the best ways I have found to allow them to see that I am real, outside of school, is to volunteer with them. For two years now, with only a few exceptions, my class has taken advantage of volunteer opportunities once a month. These are done on Saturdays, and parents are invited to help. We have done things like road and park clean ups, trail work, throwing Halloween parties and singing Christmas carols for the elderly, collecting food for the homeless, making sandwiches and stocking shelves at the food bank, and many others. This is three hours where I work alongside my students and just have a good time. We love to partner up with our local Montana Conservation Corps on their projects. I generally have between 10 to 15 students show up for each event. That is pretty good when you consider I only have 24 or 25 students overall. The students, their parents, and I all enjoy this time, and it also teaches the value of helping others.

Creating a real-world classroom is also a great way to have the students see that you are as real as they are. That is why I use the money system, because it's real. When we get caught speeding, we pay a fine. When we live in a home, we pay rent or a mortgage. When we don't show up for work, we don't get paid. When we do our job well, we get a reward (sometimes a monetary one). I also find it easier to explain my procedures to parents by using these real-world examples. When a child fails to complete his or her homework at night, it's just like when the parents don't get their work done by a deadline. There are consequences for both, generally ones that hit the good ol' pocketbook.

When I have my students line up to travel from one location to the next, I expect them to do so quietly. When they don't, I use a military tactic that works wonders. It is called about face. When I notice that they are chatting or not in a straight line, I simply say, "About face" and they know to turn around and face the other direction. I continue to say this phrase until they are quiet and ready to go. I also use the phrase, "Nose and toes." This alerts my students to check that their nose is behind someone else's head, and that their toes are pointing forward. When I say that phrase they respond by saying, "Here we go." So it sounds like this: Me: "Nose and toes." Them: "Here we go." If they are still not ready, I may say it again until they are. I also use the money system in the hallway. If they are talking, even to me, it is a standard $50 fine when they return to the classroom. It is the banker's job to remember to collect it, or he or she also owes $50.

We all know that one of the most annoying parts of being a teacher is repeating instructions more than once. I have found a foolproof way to avoid this. It is called the "Directions" cue. On the first day of the school year, I inform my students that when they hear me say the word, "Directions," they are to stop what they are doing, stand up, place their hands behind their backs, and put their eyes on me. I have discovered that when I use this procedure it is 100-percent accurate every single time. I have NEVER had a kid ask me to repeat my directions when using this tactic. It works so well, in fact, that when I forget to use it and a child asks me to repeat myself, I get very frustrated with myself for not using it. It also works great for substitutes, counselors, principals, and guest speakers. I simply tell them to say the word, "Directions," and voila . . . magically, all eyes are on them!

Showing kids that you are human is essential to making this type of teaching work. However, there are some things you need to know before you choose to make a change of this nature. First, you will find yourself in a constant state of self-reflection, almost to the point where it drives you mad. You will find faults in yourself, and you will find faults in your system. You will have to be willing to change, and you will have to be willing to become a 21st century learner. If you can't change your ways of teaching, give up control of the little things, learn to listen, share personal stuff with your students, hear and be an active participant in some pretty serious discussions, learn to trust in your students and in the concept of karma, and use a computer to teach, then this way of teaching is not going to work for you. Your own character will become your main focus so that you can properly model it for your students. I am not saying you can't have an adult life, because we all do. What I am saying is that you have to believe in what you are saying to your students. You have to allow them to see you as a human who makes mistakes. You have to model for them the act of forgiving oneself to move forward. In short, you have to be a human being.

Secondly, you will have to keep a close eye on your united classroom. Over the past three years, I have noticed that my class becomes like a family. They become extremely close and protective of one another. I especially noticed it this last year. I found that my class became too close. They were literally like brothers and sisters to one another. Now, that might not be a bad thing, but I kept hearing from specialists and the playground aides that they were arguing and picking on one another to the point of tears. So, I sat them down for a special afternoon Character Circle one day and we talked. What I came to find out was that they were so close that they were taking little things very seriously. A boy would say a pretty harmless teasing statement to a girl and the girl would treat it like it was the end of the world. What was really happening was that the little girl thought of this little boy as her brother and was appalled that he would hurt her like that. So, I had to have a pretty heavy talk about healthy teasing among siblings and how they had become so close that they had to learn to let this type of teasing go. The little boy was teasing her because he felt like he could, just as all brothers do. He thought that she knew that he would never do anything to hurt her, and that he was just having a little fun. This was a huge eye-opener for me. Who knew that a class could become too close? Wow! So, the bottom line is, you have to watch out. You have to listen to what other teachers are telling you about your students when they are not in your care. We all know that kids act differently when we are not around, but there may be more to the story than can be brought out, discussed, and solved by having a simple 10-minute meeting with your class.

As a teacher, I know what works for me. I have no clue if any of what I have presented here will work for you. My hope is that you can do what teachers do best . . . steal what sounds like it might work for you, tweak it to fit your teaching style, and then run with it. Expect failure. Expect to have to change things up. Expect that what worked this year will not work with the next group of kids the following year. I am constantly changing and rethinking what I am doing. There is nothing set in stone. I appreciate teachers that take my ideas and modify them to suit their own purposes. You are not me, and I am not you. Use what works for you in your classroom.

I would like to leave you with two concepts, however, that I do want you to steal just as they are. First, just picking up this book and thinking critically about what you have read will make you a better teacher. Second, always, always BELIEVE that you are making a difference every single day, every single hour in the lives and the hearts that you touch, even if it is only by saying hello in the hallways. Spread that belief and share your life with as many kids as you possibly can. They need us. They are dying to have us. They will remember us. They will share us, too. Just BELIEVE!

POSTSCRIPT

A Conversation

Counselors and teachers have conversations all the time about their strategies, their tactics, and their students. This book has been a conversation of sorts between us, with you as our audience. We wanted to close, however, by elaborating this process a bit, and giving you a taste of the questions that we ask each other regularly. We hope that this will help you get similar conversations started in your own school.

Tammie

What character trait do you feel is the most important for a child to master before becoming an adult? Why do you consider that trait to be so critical to the child's development?

Rusty

I'm sorry for smiling in the face of such a serious question, but I was just sitting here thinking that I haven't mastered any of the skills we talk about. I don't think about mastery when it comes to life skills, I think about growth, or even evolution, in the direction of wisdom and awareness. Having said that, I believe that self-awareness is critical to authenticity and that's the direction I like to think I'm headed in, warts and all. How about you?

Tammie

For adults, I feel that trust is the greatest foundation for human connection and relationships, but for kids I believe responsibility is most important. Society is increasingly enabling children. We need to stop solving children's problems for them. We need to allow them to fail and pick up the pieces with our encouragement. We need to allow them to see the results and benefits of being a responsible person. By the fourth grade, I expect independence. I expect them to listen and to do what I ask. When they don't, it seems like they whine and cry to their parents more and more. Then I get a call or an e-mail stating that I am a mean teacher and that their child no longer wants to come to school. My response to these parents is, "Good." That must mean that the children are taking at least a shred of responsibility and accountability for their actions. I agree with you about lifelong personal development and never really mastering these areas in our own lives, but I also believe that there are stages of mastery in each trait that we need to meet to move forward.

Here's another question for you: Do you find it hard not to take people's opinions personally?

Rusty

Yes. One of the things that made it hard to write this book was the realization that I would be criticized by some who don't agree with me. I've come to realize, however, that unless I'm making some enemies, I'm not hitting close enough to where the real issues lie. The overall health of an organization, in this case the school, has a huge effect on the outcomes of the organization, in this case test scores. Most people don't want to look at the fact that we are failing our kids when we don't live up to the very standards we expect of them. I've been in schools where half the staff doesn't even talk to one another, and they complain to the union every time an idea is advanced about needing more support on the playground or in a study hall.

One of my favorite quotes is from Teddy Roosevelt, and I repeat it to myself almost daily: "It is not the critic who counts: not the man who points out how the strong man stumbles or where the doer of deeds could have done better. The credit belongs to the man who is actually in the arena, whose face is marred by dust and sweat and blood, who strives valiantly, who errs and comes up short again and again, because there is no effort without error or shortcoming, but who knows the great enthusiasms, the great devotions, who spends himself for a worthy cause; who, at the best, knows, in the end, the triumph of high achievement, and who, at the worst, if he fails, at least he fails while daring greatly, so that his place shall never be with those cold and timid souls who knew neither victory nor defeat."

When it comes to critics, I realize that I'm not right and they're not wrong. Still, I'm the one putting myself out there, and that helps me to be less sensitive when people take shots at my ideas.

I've know you for awhile, both personally and professionally, and what has always struck me was how confident you are in the classroom. You really seem to almost become a different person when you walk through that door. Do you notice that and if so, what do you attribute that confidence to?

Tammie

That's a tough one. You have mentioned that to me before. I have always thought of myself as being a very confident person. Throughout my teaching career, however, I have gone through a lot personally to lower my self-worth and self-esteem in the "real" world. I have just recently found absolute peace in my personal life again, and slowly that real life confidence is coming back. School is not my "real" world though. There, I am the queen of the world. I am able to shine as much as the brightest star. I love every second of that life. Teaching is something I believe that I was just born to do. It is like a transformation, because it just feels natural. I don't really have to think. I am just able to go in and do it, and I get to see instant results from what I have done. I deal with kids, and they are so transparent. I don't have to guess how they are feeling, or if I am good enough to teach them. I know that what I do is making a difference in the lives of others. I feel a complete peace internally when inside those four walls. The smells, the environment, the sense of being something great all give me a sense of absolute belonging. It is where I fit in the puzzle of life.

I often wonder why I was blessed with the gift to lead and teach. I love it, and I thrive on it. I guess that is what motivates me, and I guess that my motivation could be masked as confidence.

In life we have all had to make sacrifices to get where we are today. What do you think has been your biggest sacrifice?

Rusty

Personal relationships. My mom used to worry that I was so intense and driven to find my path that I would miss the people along the way. My quest for a passionate voice and a place in the world has been all-consuming for most of my adult life. I can remember walking around alone in high school trying to figure out what my calling was and how I could use what I'd been given. Catholic guilt is a funny thing and it manifests in many ways, but for me it was a very real sense that I'd be judged based on what I did with what I'd been given. That left very little room for people who didn't share my drive for something more than average, and has left me at 48 years of age asking myself how I want to spend the next 48. I still don't suffer casual conversation very well but I'm getting better at relaxing around others. I think that's why I connect so well with kids. I see nothing but possibility in them, and I often see excuses and settling for less in people my own age. What have you had to give up?

Tammie

Empathy. I know that may sound weird coming from a teacher, especially one that just finished writing an entire book about character traits, but it is true. Somewhere along the road of life, I heard so many excuses and sad stories that I became immune to feeling sorry for others. It took a long time, years, for me to realize that this had happened. When I did, it smacked me in the face. I remember the day that I asked to talk to our school counselor. I just started crying and told him that I had lost the power and the desire to be empathetic to others. It took me forever to gain it back, and honestly, I still have days where I have to remind myself to really listen to others. I have to actually talk my way through the process at times. The good news is, I see it and I know that I need to work on it. Character building is a never-ending lesson.

When you were a child, what did you want to do when you grew up?

Rusty

I always wanted to work with people but I had a hard time figuring out exactly what that was going to look like. I wasn't one of those kids who "knew." My path has become clearer the further along I've travelled. I've been a bartender off and on since college and now I'm a counselor. I tell people it's the same job, just different hours. I guess the short answer would be I've always wanted to be Rusty.

Did you always want to be a teacher?

Tammie

Although my goals in life went on bird walks every once in awhile, I always knew that I was destined to be a teacher. During summers when I was a kid, my sister and I would ride our bikes to the school grounds. I remember one year we were looking in the garbage dumpsters. Although the reason for our behavior is lost in the mists of time, I do recall what we found: teacher's editions of textbooks. You know, the ones with the spirals on the side and all the answers in them. We felt like we had hit the jackpot. We climbed in and took all that we could find. My mom has often told me how she was always amazed that we would go to school all day and then come home and play school all night. That is how we did our homework: We would teach it. We had amazing classrooms in the basement. There was so much creativity and mimicking in those years. I was born to be a teacher. Back then I was Mrs. Crabtree, and now I am Ms. Erickson, but actually there's not a whole lot of difference between the two. I still love to look at the teacher's editions of textbooks and, believe it or not, I actually enjoy just sitting at my teacher's desk and taking it all in. It was just the other day, while giving a spelling test, that I realized that my dreams had come true. I am a teacher. I succeeded in that goal. It is who I am, and it defines me as a person. So, yes Rusty, I always, always wanted to be a teacher.

As an adult, what do you see yourself doing when you grow up? In other words, what will the next adventure or chapter of your life look like?

Rusty

I'm going to let go of who I used to be and I'm going to invest myself in others. I want to be involved in their evolution. I want to be a resource for people who are looking to make something out of what they've been given. I want to add a sentence to the dialogue, stop the endless navel gazing, and become a part of the society around me. I want to outgrow my weaknesses and contribute something to what others are doing. I've spent enough time figuring out who I am to allow myself to be available to others. You know what else? I'd like to be a dad. What do you still want to accomplish?

Tammie

I now dream of becoming a renowned speaker. I have always loved speaking in front of people, and I especially enjoy teaching others how to implement character education in the everyday classroom routine. I am unable to pursue this goal right now due to the responsibilities that come with being a mom, but I think that it is out there for me in the future. It is just that important to me. For now, I will continue to present information to small groups locally.

On another topic, what advice can you give teachers who are at their wits' end with the "modern" student?

Rusty

I am humbled that you ask me that question, and as always, I defer to you when it comes to the boots on the ground in the classroom. However, I will say that we first need to be more connected to them as people, and then, we need to be more flexible when it comes to expectations. I recently went to the Design School at Stanford University and toured their facility. What jumped out at me was the lack of desks and chairs; there was an abundance of open space and white boards everywhere. What furniture they did have was all on wheels so it could be easily moved into whatever configuration the group felt was needed. The D School, as it's called, finds that creative thinking and learning is not a passive activity and that students do better when they can move around and interact with each other and the information. I believe we are moving in that direction in the K-12 environment as the classroom becomes more fluid and interactive. Some of the old rules about what "good" student behaviors look like need to be rewritten. I've read several articles that talk about letting students lay on the floor when they do their work, and to encourage small group discussions and collaboration as much as possible. We need to set high expectations for ourselves and our students that are consistent with the reality of our situation today.

You are in the classroom every day and I know that this year's class has been a unique challenge. Can you define the issues that you're dealing with and how you make progress with the "modern" student?

Tammie

First of all, I completely agree with you: We are teaching the future, and the future is coming so rapidly that the lessons that I teach my kids today will likely be out-of-date very quickly. However, one constant that will always remain is the need for character education. Kids are not prepared for the future in this area, and teachers, counselors, parents, and administrators that ignore this deficit are doing every child that comes into their orbit a huge disservice. One thing that frustrates me, especially this year, is the fact that I have to spend six weeks undoing all the bad habits that prior influences have placed on my students. Allowing them to slack off in their homework, allowing excuses such as, "Well, he has a rough home life," and allowing students to think of themselves as equals with adults, rather than learning respectful boundaries, makes my job much harder.

This year has been exceptionally challenging. In fact, it's probably been the most challenging in my 10 years of teaching. This set of kids includes many that lack social and character skills. They use phrases like, "Get that off my desk," that are just hurtful to others. Generally, you have one or two kids that need special attention in these types of areas, but when it's more than half of your class, you feel that you lose the teaching aspect of your job and become a motivational speaker. More and more pressure is placed on the teacher to make huge academic gains in 180 days of school. It takes a tough teacher to ignore those pressures and realize that it is not the academics that are going to move a student from the immaturity of childhood into an active participant in society. All children can learn. They will learn for the rest of their lives, and much of that learning will be self-taught as an adult. Let's face it, the stuff we teach is important, but we NEVER go into in the depth needed to move a skill to long-term memory. Why do you think we teach addition, subtraction, nouns, the planets, etc., etc., etc., every single year, over and over and over again?

In all honesty the knowledge a child will or will not retain depends on that child's interests. That is why in college you get to choose classes that interest you. It is the drive and the motivation inside the child's heart that is important. We are there to share what we know with them. We spark their interest, and we start to form their dreams of becoming firefighters, police officers, bakers, construction workers, lawyers, doctors, farmers, and teachers . . . all by giving them little snippets of topics that they may like to look into more closely. What they really take with them is the desire, the want, to move forward and be successful, and make those dreams a reality. Our real job is to instill in them the power to believe in themselves, and eventually in others.

So, that is what I am doing this year. I am forming relationships with the students and their families. I am taking it one day at a time. I am not taking their faults personally, and I am giving grace to those that need it. At the same time, I am raising expectations, encouraging solutions rather than excuses, and learning to hug. I am not a hugger, and by the fourth grade I feel that hugs are overrated. However, this year, I need to just take time to hug them and allow the love of a teacher to flow through my arms. They just need them for some reason. They need to know that their teacher believes in them, every single day.

On occasion this year, I have reviewed my class list name by name to remind myself of where those kids were when they walked through that door, and how far they have come. Now that the year is closing, it has changed. Earlier, I was ready to throw in the towel. I had literally exhausted all the tricks in my bag. Then, magically, it all clicked. This has absolutely been my most challenging year of teaching, but it has also been one of the best of my career! I have seen amazing things happen in the lives of 21 children this year, academically as well as socially. I hung in there until the end, and I am once again blessed with the knowledge that just when you think there is nothing left to give, you dig deeper and find another way. Kids are just that special.

In short, Rusty, I am ignoring the politicians and doing my part to transform the "modern" student into an adult who has an idea of what life can be, for today as well as tomorrow.

Rusty

Well, on that inspiring note, I'll say "Goodnight Gracie." I can't tell you how much I appreciate you for being my partner in this effort. Even more, I thank you for being my friend and ally in this fight for the hearts and the minds of our students, and our future.

Tammie

Back at you my friend. Back at ya!

Read-Aloud Books Used to Teach Character in Ms. Erickson's Classroom

Citizenship

Barack Obama Out of Many, One by Shana Corey
BO America's Commander In Leash by Naren Aryal
A Flug For Our Country by Eve Spencer
America is . . . by Louise Borden
Miss Rumphius by Barbara Cooney

Responsibility

No Excuses by Dr. Wayne W. Dyer
Pirates Don't Change Diapers by Melinda Long

Respect

Chrysanthemum by Kevin Henkes
Whoever You Are by Mem Fox
Whoopi's Big Book or Manners by Whoopi Goldberg
Chicken Fingers, Mac and Cheese . . . Why Do You Always Have To Say Please by Wendy Rosen and Jackie End

Trustworthiness

The Honest-to-Goodness Truth by Patricia C. McKissack

Fairness
Michaels's Golden Rules by Deloris Jordan

Courage
Courage by Bernard Waber
Riding Freedom by Pam Muñoz Ryan

Caring
Petey by Ben Mikaelsen

REFERENCES

[1] American School Counselor Association, Alexandria, Virginia, as sourced through U.S. Department of Education, Common Core of Data, National Institute for Educational Statistics—Public Elementary and Secondary School Student Enrollment and Staff from the Common Core of Data: School Year 2008-2009 (www.schoolcounselor.org/content.asp?contentid=460).

[2] Kriete, Roxann, *The Morning Meeting Book*, Northeast Foundation for Children, 2002 (www.responsiveclassroom.org/product/morning-meeting book).

[3] Palmer, Parker J., *The Courage to Teach: Exploring the Inner Landscape of a Teacher's Life*, Jossey-Bass, 1997, pp 10 (www.amazon.com/Courage-Teach-Exploring-Landscape-Teachers/dp/0787910589).

[4] Ginott, Haim, *Teacher and Child: A Book for Parents and Teachers*, AVON Books, 1972 (www.amazon.com/Teacher-Child-Book-Parents-Teachers/dp/0380003236).

[5] Character Camp Newspaper Article in the Billings Gazette: http://billingsgazette.com/news/local/article_0ce02774-c597-5829-a6e1-d0503271f8e6.html

[6] Grotberg, Edith, "Countering Depression with the Five Building Blocks of Resilience," *Reaching Today's Youth*, Vol. 4, No. 1 (Fall 1999), pp. 66-72 (www.cyc-net.org/Journals/rty-4-1.html).

7   Glasser, William, *Choice Theory: A New Psychology of Personal Freedom*, Harper, 1998 (www.amazon.com/exec/obidos/ASIN/0060191090/wfurrcom-20).

8   www.justice.gov/dea/ongoing/red_ribbon/redribbon_history.html.